PERMISSION GRANTED

*From Who I've Been
to Who I'm Becoming*

CANDICE WEST

LANDON
HAIL
PRESS

Paperback ISBN: 978-1-959955-45-0
Hardback ISBN: 978-1-959955-46-7

Cover design by Rich Johnson, Spectacle Photo
Photography by Angelli Nguyen
Creative Direction by Brittany Barcellos, BXB Productions
Published by Landon Hail Press

Disclaimer: The views and opinions presented herein are those of the author and do not represent or reflect the views, policy, or positions of the Department of Defense (DoD) or its Components. Appearance of, or reference to, any commercial products or services does not constitute DoD endorsement of those products or services. The appearance of external hyperlinks does not constitute DoD endorsement of the linked websites, or the information, products or services therein.

This is a work of creative nonfiction. All of the events in this collection are true to the best of the author's memory. Some names and identifying features may have been changed to protect the identity of certain parties. The author in no way represents any company, corporation, or brand, mentioned herein. The views expressed in this collection are solely those of the authors.

Content Warning: This book contains potentially triggering subject matter, including, but not limited to, discussions of past trauma, flashbacks of child abuse (emotional and mental), death of a parent, domestic violence, sexual assault, addiction, and PTSD. Proceed only if you are comfortable with potentially sensitive topics.

To my kids, this is your permission slip to live fully and authentically in your essence. And in living we don't always get it right. Should you ever feel shame, doubt, or fear, come back here. Here is where you will be reminded that we can rise from anything if we give ourselves permission, choose ourselves, and do *the work.* Love, Mom

To those who have felt too much, not enough, and everything in between: I see you, I am you, and I witness you. My hope is that you read this with curiosity, use my stories as your permission slip to release shame, guilt, and any heavy feelings you harbor. To connect back to self and live in your personal power—join in the #meera movement. In Gratitude, Candice

Advance Praise for *Permission Granted*

"In this day and age of inauthentic highlight reels online, ten-second videos, and quick clips into people's real lives, it's so refreshing to take an authentic deep dive into Candice's personal journey. We all have so many layers and instances in life that shape us. Her vulnerable rehashing of her own journey draws you in and helps you see that no matter your circumstances, there can be healing and the ability to pivot to find your best self.

"As I wound through this book I not only got a deeper glimpse into the (beautifully written) story of the author—whom I have come to know, respect, and value—I also got to reflect on how my own story and life events have shaped how I show up in the world and engage with the prompts and reflection points spread throughout the book.

"I highly recommend this book if you are on your own healing journey, want to deepen self-awareness, or even just want to feel more connected to an authentic story on the messy evolution of a beautiful human."

—Chelsea Fournier
Founder & Business Strategist
at Intuitive Business By Design

"It's been my honor to witness Candice on her journey within to return to herself. Sharing her own pivotal experiences and potent reclamation of personal power, she illuminates the path of possibility and guides you back to your heart. *Permission Granted*—part memoir, part operating manual—is a compass you can recalibrate to again and again."

—Nancy Levin
Bestselling Author
of *Embrace Your Shadow to Find Your Light*

"In Candice West's *Permission Granted*, Candice takes us on a poignant journey through her own life, both the pain and the triumph. Through each event, the reader is powerfully shown how to accept all aspects of one's life and cultivate a better tomorrow."

—Christine Fonseca
Bestselling Author, Speaker, Consultant, & Coach

Table Of Contents

Introduction

Fertilizer, though literally made of shit, is used to nourish plants of all kinds. Though disgusting on its own, it can be transformed and used to support growth and beauty. Imagine a world without trees, plants, or flowers. Look at all the benefits they give us and the connection we feel as we watch them sprout and take on new life each season.

Now imagine replacing that plant, tree, or flower with your own existence. By feeding yourself new forms of nourishment, how different would your seasons look? Visualize the beauty in your transformation just as you would view the beauty of a blossoming flower.

Blooming from a survival-state into a thrive-state can be done in this lifetime, if you give yourself permission. I have done it, my clients have done it, my family and friends have done it. And we will do it over and over again through the many seasons we will navigate. Much like the use of fertilizer, we use our own personal shit as lessons, as guideposts forward, allowing us to grow, shift, and transform into who we have always been meant to be.

This book is your permission slip to look into your past, present, and future. Though you don't need *my* permission to do it, if you are like me and have felt shame (and maybe even guilt or denial) for seasons in your life, you might welcome that invitation. So before reading further, take this "now moment" to reflect on your life choices up to this point. See where each path has led you in your personal evolution, and see where you have overlooked recurring themes and patterns, maybe even resulting in self-sabotage and self-abandonment. Notice how others have hurt you and how you have hurt others. And if it feels aligned, you might just take a moment to notice what needs you were meeting in those seasons.

Speaking of this "now moment," I use this phrase to bring me back to the present. There is the present moment, and then there is each moment within the present. Remembering this phrase allows me to hold on tightly and cherish it however it is presented.

You see, it is all in self-awareness. As you continue reading, you will read all about my storms and earthquakes, and you will learn how my deeply-rooted beliefs led me to subconsciously sabotage what could have otherwise been some beautiful seasons in my life. But, because we know life happens *for* us not *to* us, the small pivots matter, and I know it all had to happen and unfold in exactly this way.

Friends, it is time to choose differently. It is time to give yourself permission to show up and live this one life you were gifted. And it is time to give yourself permission to release the shame, guilt, and other pain you store subconsciously, as a way of punishing yourself for your wrongdoings.

I will be sharing some of the lived experiences that really shaped my personal belief system as a child and led me to the adult version–the toxic and unhealthy version–of Candice. Now this is not me bashing myself, as I love all versions of Candice; rather, it's knowing what I used to be versus what I am now. Having done *the work*, I now know, understand, and accept the difference.

I encourage you to read without judgment because you might find yourself in my stories, and judging me is judging you. Plus, judging is not helpful when attempting to transform ourselves. Judgment is a frequency that keeps us in a state of comparison and separation. Instead, I encourage you to read from a place of curiosity. I ask you to understand that this is the result of many years of trauma, followed by many years of doing *the work*. I encourage you to read to become familiar with the power of belief systems in affecting day stacked upon day and generation stacked upon generation. As you read, I encourage you to find compassion for those you love or dislike.

Read again and again if you need to.

Each era takes you along my personal and intimate journey. It reveals most of my truths and may help you to understand your own thoughts, actions, and behaviors, both in hindsight and in this present now moment. It gives you permission to see your garden for what it is. Whether overrun by weeds or in full bloom, as our seasons change, so does our garden. Don't judge what it looks like in this now moment; remember, we are *forever in bloom*.

The Awakening Era

"Awakening means you've come home to yourself, that consciousness has shifted back to its original nature."

—Maria Eming

This is familiar. This is all too familiar, I thought to myself one work night after cocktails and television with Keith. We headed to bed, going through our nightly routine, locking everything up, setting alarms, and plumping pillows so our heads would bury into them as we laid down. He placed his CPAP on his face, lay flat on his back with his hands laced together, and drifted off into his dreams. I, on the other hand, acknowledged it was another night—now clocking a solid ten months—since we had been intimate or I had received any physical touch. I rolled over on my left side to help silence the gasps of air I would take from holding my bellows and deep belly cries inside, wondering what happened. Wondering how we ended up here.

Entering the rabbit hole of all the possible *whys* of why my husband was so different. Why it seemed he did not desire intimacy, affection—you know, the things that distinguish a marriage from a friendship. He seemed to avoid me all together. It felt like we were roommates. I went from that rabbit hole to the next one, in deep curiosity as to why we were drinking so much. It seemed with each duty station it became more frequent with more consumed. Following the late night drinking were the trips to the pantry to help dry up the alcohol and fulfill the sugar and carb cravings the alcohol gave us. *How is this my life?* I asked myself. *I have worked my entire life to NOT be like my parents, and here I am living out a piece of both their worlds.*

Lying in bed crying, I felt so miserable. So disconnected from my spouse, from myself. I remember wondering if this was life as a mom and wife, three kids deep, dual active duty, and living overseas. Is this what everyone talks about... you know... the woman forgetting herself, losing herself trying to be *the thing* to and for everyone else? I felt selfish for even considering that because I knew all too well what it was like to feel emotionally neglected, abandoned, and alone as a child. To feel invisible in a room full of people who are supposed to love and care for you. And I knew I would be willing to give all of myself if that meant none of my family had to feel what I felt.

Of course work would be the next rabbit hole into which my mind would take me. Family and work was all I knew; we didn't really have friends—Keith and Candice all the way, every day. They say leadership is lonely at the top, and I would not disagree. I gave so much to work. The one thing that made me feel somewhat worthy, content, and like I mattered was my work. I had always excelled at my job regardless of where they assigned me, but this place was different. I seemed to be the odd ball out. It seemed I was purposely planted at this location to allow me to see all versions of myself across all timelines. Like they each held up a mirror all at once. It was too much all at once, so denial felt safest. I didn't enjoy work, I didn't always enjoy the people, I didn't always enjoy the leadership. And the rules, my goodness, all the rules—I didn't enjoy them. It made the days long, hard, and dark. I questioned myself, always. This was my sense of worthiness, and without that, I felt nothing.

And like clockwork... the next rabbit hole: Dad. The self-talk of how much he cared for all my other siblings more than me. How he showed more care and compassion for my sister Jennifer, who was not even his biological child, more support and encouragement for my brother Herbert because he was the star athlete, and how much I felt he babied my youngest sister, Elise. How much I felt like the scapegoat, always the one blamed and at fault. I spoke and was misunderstood, laughed and was too loud. Just taking up space felt wrong.

The last rabbit hole was my mom. This rabbit hole always seemed to surface last, even though a significant amount of my childhood abuse took place under her roof... maybe because I felt pity for her and all she endured as a child, maybe because she stuck it out and did the best she could, maybe because of the codependency we shared and how she now treated me as an adult, but more than likely a blend if it all. I found myself trying to understand how a mother can neglect her children in so many ways. How I didn't ask to come into this world, yet there I was, navigating horrendous experiences because she chose to not do *the work*. Wondering how I deserved all the abuse, I laid there, fed up. Fed up with feeling this way. Fed up with drinking, with eating my feelings, with blaming everyone else for my current state of misery.

These thoughts circulated and circulated. All of them, repeated, and repeated, and repeated. Tears flowing, body shaking as my victim mindset was fully activated. I remember thinking it was not fair. Not only did my Dad not show me love, affection, or attention, but here I am in a relationship mirroring that same thing. I guess I am not worthy of any of it. *What is wrong with me?* I thought. I need to fix this, fix me.

And then it hit me. I have always said people come into our lives for a reason, a season, or a lifetime. There was a 70-year-old woman I knew in my life; her name was Greta, and we had met at a work event. Her personality was so bubbly and friendly, you couldn't help but be pulled into her energy. Well, the relationship morphed over the years into a friendly one where we kept in touch. But as I got to know her, the bubbly friendly traits seemed more superficial, a mask she wore giving the illusion of being happy. I saw that side of her less and less and noticed it was replaced with what felt like victim energy. She would quickly take over any and all conversations and it would become storyhour where she shared the woes of her childhood. Over the years I knew her, the same ones played on repeat, making it difficult not only to want to be around her but also to show her empathy. *C'mon, time to move on* were my thoughts.

That is when it hit me. Candice, what you don't change, you choose. Greta is a mirror. She is you, and you are she. You are triggered by her woe-is-me because that is in you. That is the piece you are avoiding healing, moving through. You are holding onto it like a childhood toy you refuse to let go of. *But why?* I asked myself in deep and utter confusion. *That is how you show up in conversation with your sister Jennifer. That is the mindset you have while in conversation with your Dad.* I remember thinking at that moment, now crying even harder, that I did not want to become that. But the following thought was, *I already was and am.* I didn't want people to *not* want to be around me because I was still telling stories of the past. More importantly, I didn't want to keep telling the stories. I was tired. Tired of the tears, tired of feeling empty, tired of clinging to the stories only for them to reinforce my beliefs. I felt like a volcano erupting. Realizing what I had become, I immediately resorted to shaming myself... no wonder my husband doesn't desire me, no wonder he drinks all the time. Hell, no wonder I drink all the time, reinforcing that deep-seated belief: *I am too much.*

I pulled myself out of bed and walked into the living room. I remember saying out loud, "God, what do I do? I am so tired of feeling this way. Feeling like I don't matter, like I am not good enough. I am tired of carrying all this weight. I am tired of drinking. I don't know what to do. I am just tired. I just need a break from the chaos and you just bring me more. I need a sign, I need some help." Little did I know in that now moment that this was a form of surrender. As much as I resisted it, I was cracking open. And what I have learned is: *"what we resist, persists"*- Carl Jung. I was starting unconsciously to surrender what I knew to be true. I wiped my face and nose, now all stuffy, and I opened my cell phone to scroll. And there it was. A fellow beachbody coach who was now a spiritual mindset coach—was this my sign? Spiritual mindset. *Hmmm,* I thought. In true Candice fashion, I filled out the application right away. Impulsivity or a *knowing*? I wouldn't know until I filled it out and submitted it. In this moment, which I remember exactly, I thought to myself, *Something has to change. It has to be me.* I have always had a fear of turning out like my parents. I have always worried about becoming them. I wondered for a brief moment if I had. I sat on the couch, still calming the internal storm I had just experienced, filling out the intake form as I wiped my tears and the snot that trickled down my nose. I was giving myself permission for whatever was to come next.

I fell asleep crying like I did many nights. I woke the next morning tired with puffy red eyes but a fire lit within me. I was confused. I didn't know how to be. For some reason in my mind, having this newfound awareness from the night before, I felt like I should just be able to change and shift. Voila… and so it is—hahaha. I also couldn't help but wonder what was happening to me and why now. Why is this the moment in time where I am being challenged to unravel all these years? In this process of facing my truth, I got real honest with myself. I recognized that over the years I was self-soothing with food, alcohol, work, and any other distraction I could find to keep me from avoiding feeling. To remain strong and in control. And here, I felt like I was losing control. How was it that this duty station was breaking me?

I am built for hard.

I am built for chaos.

I am built to endure abuse.

Ego swooped in and took over. I was not going to be defeated. Surrendering to this after all I have been through translates to: I am weak. It means I am broken. It means I am not strong. Strong is how I have survived. Strong is how I have made it through. Strong is the only way. *But how do I get back my strength? How do I find it again?*

What an adventure the next few years would be, awakening me to a depth I didn't know I was ready for. In all the times prior when I attempted change, I pulled weed by weed, day by day. But nothing seemed to stick for long. I would soon revert back to old ways of living, thinking, and behaving. What I didn't realize or understand back then was that, just like in a garden, weeds grow back; it is not until you grab it at its root that it is permanently gone.

Challenging me beyond my comfort zone. Launching me into new visions, perspectives, and knowings. Discovering hidden truths I was not even able to admit to myself for many years following. And deep intense feelings, sensations, and communication from within my body, resulting in medical challenges that spoke to me: *it was time.* It was time to dig in, take a deep and hard look at myself, and do *the work.*

I lost and found myself all in the same tour. And this was just the beginning. The beginning of something heavy, disheartening, frustrating, while also, enlightening, healing, and expansive. As my mentor, Jen, says: *You have to live forward to understand it in reverse.* So, let's reverse and rewind so you can understand with more clarity just how this version of Candice was created and who she morphed into because of it all. It was this very version of me that could no longer exist in this way. I suddenly saw life differently and felt everything around me was crumbling—it was like an earthquake measuring a ten on the Richter scale.

PERMISSION GRANTED to acknowledge your awakening, embrace your truth, and honor your journey of transformation.

The Formative Era

"People raised on love see things differently than those raised on survival."

—Joy Marino

Tumultuous. Toxic. Traumatic. These are the words that come to mind when I think back to my childhood. Looking at parenting through my eyes, as a grown woman and adult, I cannot wrap my head around any of it. Although, I suppose if I am being honest with myself, I can see some semblance of where I was headed: straight into the path of the same tornado.

Going back as far as I can remember, there was always this story of me at nine months old. I was in the hospital, undergoing tests; my dad always made it sound so life threatening. It wasn't until I was older, in my early forties, that I received the medical record my mom had kept and I fully learned and understood: I was diagnosed with failure to thrive. A variety of things can cause this, but for me, it was because I wasn't eating. The pediatricians swapped out formulas, did a plethora of testing, and performed many different evaluations with no definitive resolution, until finally, it just passed. My mom believes it was because I got all my teeth in at once so I became uninterested–pain, swollen gums, crankiness… all the typical things that follow teething. I share this to show that even at less than a year old, it appears as if I was *too much*. My five other siblings didn't require hospital stays. Numerous appointments taking mom away from work. Special food and monitors. Ripping the family apart, having to move across the world to be in closer proximity to the specialists, as we were currently stationed in Bermuda at the Navy base. Little did I know how that would play out over my lived experience. How an energetic seed would be planted–by all those hospital stays, doctor visits, family exchanges–in my physical body, watering over and over the subconscious belief, *I am too much*.

By the time I was two years old, my parents ended up getting divorced. My dad remained in California with his new partner, and we eventually moved to Ohio with my mom as she also moved onto her next relationship. I don't have any memories during this time at all. I have been told my dad eventually got stationed in California, where we were still able to see him. It was a summer BBQ and again, with my desire to inquire and be adventurous, along with a likely desire to disobey, I wound up sitting in the bottom of a pool where a man by the name of Squeeze jumped in and saved me. (As you continue to read, you will learn that, throughout the course of my life, there have been a few times death was knocking on my doorstep.)

As you can see, from the very beginning I liked to live life on my terms, challenging authority and finding out the hard way. From a young age I seemed to crave all life's experiences, but as a result, I also got to face their consequences.

A few years later, my siblings, my mom, my stepfather, and I were living on Rose Avenue in Norwalk, Ohio. Each day seemed like *Groundhog Day*. I remember being in tap dance and gymnastics, dancing and singing in the living room to JAM. On weekends, we spent our time outside, playing on the swing set or playing Red Rover or hide-and-seek with the neighborhood kids. Although I had friends in the neighborhood, I struggled a lot to connect and feel accepted at school. I looked different—I had buck teeth, a large gap between my front two teeth, frizzy hair, and freckles, and when I smiled, my nose scrunched up and looked like a pig snout. This affected my self-esteem and kept me from putting myself out there. The fear of rejection was fierce. So, most days I played by myself on the monkey bars and walked around singing in my head, doing cartwheels and front flips. That, or I played with the other kids usually targeted by the bullies. Throughout those years, I created stories in my mind that were watering the seed that I just *wasn't enough*.

At home, us siblings played a lot and fought a lot, and we definitely noticed an uptick in fighting between our parents. They always thought we couldn't hear them, but we could. We would just keep playing house and school while locked up in the attic playroom, distracting ourselves from the yelling and name-calling happening below us. Before we knew it, we were moving, *again*.

Drowning in a sadness of wanting what others had, some of what I thought were essentials, I was told, "Be grateful for what you have; someone else out there has it worse." It was not that I was not grateful for what I had. It just seemed to me that something was a little off in how we lived and connected with the world around us.

My mom and her husband separated and we started living just the five of us crammed in a small—very small—apartment. I can still see it. The front door with a narrow entryway, making a left that led into a long narrow hall. Off to the left a little ways down was the kitchen, and to the right a little further down was the bedroom all four kids shared. I cannot believe our two sets of big wooden bunk beds fit in that one room! Toward the front of the apartment were two other rooms. There was the living room, and a large room for my mom to fit her ginormous waterbed and bedroom set.

We faced heavy challenges in that apartment. I remember one evening my stepfather was over and he and my mom had gotten into an argument. I always found myself in the middle of these events; I felt like I needed to be there. Maybe it was a sense of control because life always felt so unpredictable. Maybe it was a need to protect my mom or be a cheerleader on the side. I remember so vividly being in the kitchen. Lots of yelling and screaming, name-calling, and colorful words filled the apartment. My stepfather was facing me and my mom. They kept going back and forth, and I remember feeling stuck in the middle, literally. Then he pulled a large butcher knife on my mom. In my mind, it was a threat to kill her. As a small child under the age of ten, why would I think anything else? Meanwhile, my mom was standing behind me with a pair of scissors, threatening him in return. I remember feeling as if I was a buffer between the two. I stood there frozen, unable to move or speak. My heart raced, rapid breaths almost like I was going to hyperventilate, but you couldn't see it on the outside. Tunnel vision. Ears muffled but capable of making out each word clearly. Confusion. *Do I take the knife, do I stand still, do I run? Legs, why are you not running, why are you not removing me from this situation?*

The event felt so long and drawn out. In reality it probably lasted a minute, maybe two. But the impact was lifelong. This event planted a seed and belief that I would spend this lifetime watering, that *I am not safe*. It was created and formed by my body's physiological response to the event. My thoughts that immediately followed: *What is happening? That butcher knife will really make her bleed. What if he hurts me, too? I can't call 911—we do not have a phone.* I had watched movies with scenes mirroring this experience, and it actually felt like we were in one. To tell you what happened after that moment is impossible. What I do know is that soon after, they were no longer married.

Their divorce process wasn't a pleasant time. They fought about everything, even the exchange of child visitation. Mom was working a lot. We were very poor, lived on food stamps and welfare, and our home always seemed to be infested with bugs. I will never forget getting ready for school and turning on the bathroom light to find a cockroach hanging on the bristles of my toothbrush. After it scurried off when the light turned on, I remember closing my eyes to brush my teeth and convincing myself the toothpaste on the top of the bristles would clean its germs before hitting my mouth. This was just how we lived. It was our normal. It was all I knew.

Adjusting to the environment of home, I was also challenged with my stepfather no longer wanting to see me. In a new relationship, his new girlfriend was not a fan of him remaining connected to his non-biological kids, so he made a choice—her over us. Not only did this water the seed, *I was not enough*, but it also planted a new one, *I am unlovable*.

Fast forward with me a moment into my adulthood. I decided to attend therapy and started trauma work using a modality called EMDR (Eye Movement Desensitization and Reprocessing). I remember having to navigate my way to the root of feeling unlovable. There were many layers stacked on top, each of which I had thought was the root, only to pull it out, heal from it, and discover a deeper seeded one: abandonment from a father figure after he had moved on from my mother. Being surrounded by someone everyday for years and losing them overnight was hard to wrap my head around.

I questioned many things about the situation. I remember him coming back to the house one weekend to pick up my other two sisters, his biological daughters. I opened my door to see him standing there. He said, "Hi, I am here to pick up Danielle and Trichia." I remember looking him dead in the eye and shouting, *"BASTARD!"* I remember saying it with such anger and deep pain, and then him staring back at me speechless. I didn't understand why I was so easily discarded.

I remember feeling so hurt and confused; I wondered what was wrong with me. I thought I had done something wrong. I remember asking myself out loud in the bathroom one morning when I was doing my hair for school, "If someone loves you, how do they just leave you?" Almost like I was expecting God to whisper a response that would justify it, making all the pain dissipate.

As I continued moving through life, I found myself taking on the caregiver role. Though we had a sitter, and then another sitter, and then another, it revolved so quickly that before we knew it, my sister Jennifer and I had taken on the role. I took on the extra duty of "housemaid," too. I chuckle as I say this because while yes, children should have chores, I remember clear as day using Murphy's Oil, the end of a fork, and a washcloth to clean the crevices of my mom's dining room table. I always felt like that was a little above and beyond normal household chores, and dreaded actually becoming an adult if this was its truth.

I was now in junior high school, and we had moved again and again due to evictions. At this point we were living on Perry Street, in Sandusky, Ohio. My typical day would be school, then home to work on schoolwork. I definitely was not the scholar in the family. We had so much going on at home that my grades weren't the best. I passed, but usually by memorizing what I needed to, dumping it, and then moving on to the next.

I often was compared to Jennifer, especially when it came to school and grades. And through varying circumstances, it planted another seed: *I am not smart.* I heard all the time from my mom how I didn't apply myself, and while some of that might be true, I was also helping to hold down the household, cooking, cleaning, doing laundry, and babysitting my siblings. I was distracted with the environment and certainly not focused on reading about the Civil War.

This belief stayed with me all the way through high school. In fact, the guidance counselor at my high school told me I would never get into a four-year college. I had a thirteen on the ACT and she told me I needed a minimum of an eighteen to be accepted, so not to bother and to focus on alternative options. This continued watering the seed of *I am not smart, I am not enough.* I got to a point where I would sit in my room in the evenings writing cheesy poetry and trying to figure out how I could contribute to society without being a leech.

Outside of school and grades, these were formative years in discovering myself and who I was as a person. Forming an identity. What on earth did I like, desire, want, need, feel? I felt like I was flying through the days on autopilot, just trying to get by without getting beat up at school, kicked out of class, smacked at home, and called names by my family.

The only identity I knew was the version that was *too much*. Ever feel like that? I swear I have lived an entire life of feeling *too much* while also *not being enough*.

Candice, you talk too much.

Candice, your laugh is obnoxious.

Candice, you're too opinionated.

Candice, you're eating again?

Candice, you have a big butt.

Candice, your boobs are huge.

Candice, you have great birthing hips.

Candice, you're not smart enough.

Candice, you're not skinny enough.

Candice, you're not good enough.

This came from all angles in my life: parents, sisters, friends, boys, role models, mentors, teachers. Gosh, as far back as I can remember, every report card said, *disruptive in class, talks too much.* At home, questions were not welcomed, because it was considered back talking and questioning authority. Curiosity? Not welcomed. It felt like at every stage in life, my "too muchness" was highlighted and shamed. I began to withdraw, silence myself, go along with the authority in the room in order to feel safe. Before I knew it, outside of the air I breathed, the only thing going in and out of my mouth was food.

Food: another thing in my life with which I have had a long-term love/hate relationship, starting with my failure to thrive diagnosis. I became addicted to food as a way to self-soothe in what felt like an abusive and loveless home. Food was something I could control, it tasted good, it made me feel happy. It felt safe, but at the same time, it seemed like there was never enough.

I recall many nights being woken at 1 a.m. or later to drunken arguments. Every Thursday through Sunday, my mom and her new live-in boyfriend fought so much. I am talking about things being thrown around the house, fists going through walls, lamps being launched and broken. This was a weekly ritual. I would wake shaking, then run to the stairs and watch it all unfold. I had younger sisters upstairs who would also wake up. I would be the buffer on the stairs so they couldn't come down to witness what was happening. I remember one time, it had gotten so bad I came down and jumped on my mom's boyfriend's back before trying to call 911. I would try to fall back asleep, stomach in knots, shaking, only to have to shower and head to school for the day.

This happened every week for years before she left him, only to take him back over and over again. I dreaded it. My body anticipated it. I was often sick with stomach issues, and after so many trips to the emergency room, proctologists, stool samples in the mail, and specialist upon specialist, I was diagnosed with irritable bowel syndrome (IBS) freshman year of high school. Chronic stress had morphed into anxiety, which had evolved into irritable bowel syndrome.

My childhood alone is a book I could write. Keeping it simple, looking at Maslow's Hierarchy of Needs, we never exceeded the bottom tier of the pyramid—one's basic needs being met.

My friends' families were different, and I tried to be around them every chance I got. I truly felt like some of the families I clung to were God's earth angels. We laughed, talked, went to church, and had dinners together at the table. It was like I was trying to be shown acceptance and unconditional love. Maybe even what was *normal*... but really, even as an adult, I ask myself, *What is normal?* I know without a doubt what I experienced was abnormal.

PERMISSION GRANTED to rewrite my story with compassion and love.

The Masked Era

Journal Entry - 1996 (Entry from 16 year old Candice)

Things happen and we don't know why -
We feel so alone and want to curl up and cry -
We feel blamed for things that aren't really our fault -
But it's guilt we feel, and like the size of a grain of salt -
Hopefully, someday we will overcome this feeling -
Maybe then someday our hearts will start healing –

We all want to be innately loved for the truth of who we are. Without conditions, without judgment and criticism. Without feeling the need to wear masks, shapeshift, and bend to the room. When we don't fear being judged or losing loved ones, our job, and friendships, we feel safer to show up as our authentic selves. But when we fear these things, we lose ourselves along the way, trying to show up in ways that will be accepted or help us to feel a sense of safety. Love is so rooted in the depth of our heart and soul that as it becomes tainted and scarred, it almost feels unrepairable. To feel love and connection is a privilege. I say that because some have been so deeply affected by their experiences that they wear armor as a way to self-protect. But as the armor protects them from the pain, it also blocks others' love from permeating deep inside.

Growing up in a home with several siblings and a single mother, I quickly became responsible for things, as the military would say, "outside my paygrade." I can remember cooking pot roast meals at nine years old, riding my bike miles to and from the bank to deposit my mom's cash from her bartending shift the night before, buying her cigarettes at age ten with a written permission slip, and walking a mile to and from the grocery store to do major grocery shopping.

These responsibilities at such a young age confused me. I wasn't sure how I was supposed to act. I was a mixture of child, teenager, and adult. I was like a robot programmed to behave and conduct herself depending on who she was around. And I can't discount when adults told me I was so well-behaved and mature for my age; it reinforced that the way I was presenting was "good."

At home I cleaned, cooked, and ran errands, while also singing, playing my violin, and feeling left out from what others my age were doing. But I was still ridiculed, criticized, judged, and constantly projected on by parents who assumed I was behaving as they once did. My mom even directed Jennifer to rummage through my bookbag, searching for anything she could find, mainly looking for drugs and cigarettes.

I was also preemptively *taught a lesson*. It was my youngest sister Trichia's birthday, and my other sister, Danielle, and I went to the convenient store for a few things my mom had on a list. Turns out Danielle stole a piece of candy. When we got home, my mother called the city's juvenile detention center and had both Danielle and I sent there as "unruly" children. She was upset my sister had stolen something and wanted her to learn her lesson. She made me go along as a scare tactic so I wouldn't make the bad choices she assumed I was making. She also said I had a *mouth on me* and this would set me straight.

I struggled to process what was happening. How was I a bad kid? I didn't drink, smoke, or do drugs, and wasn't sexually active. I was involved in school extracurriculars and got acceptable grades, but here I was being sent to a juvenile detention center, placed in a rubber room to be taught a lesson for a behavior that had never happened.

Danielle and I sat in that room for what felt like hours. *What did I do? Why is it that when my siblings get in trouble I always get clumped in with them?* I felt damned if I did, and damned if I didn't. I also remember thinking to myself, *No one loves me.* This was not the first time these thoughts ran through my mind. It happened more often than not.

Finally we were released, my mom and her boyfriend picked us up, and we went straight to Trichia's birthday party. We were expected to just be okay, cheerful, and in the birthday spirit. I planted a smile on my face, ate my feelings, and never talked about it again.

Moving forward, the safest thing was to create my masks and wear them. I showed people what I felt safe showing them. And that changed daily. What I did know to be true was I had to be "good." It wasn't safe to make mistakes. It wasn't safe to ask questions. This made me so hypervigilant. I was skilled at anticipating the next, and the next, and the next. It was exhausting. Constantly scanning my environment, people's energy, and their moods, I was always prepared with numerous plans of action so I didn't upset anyone. In the instances where I accidentally did make someone angry, I was guilted and shamed. Then, of course, I also guilted and shamed myself for not being as forward thinking as I thought I should have been.

These behaviors propelled me into living and conducting myself as a young child with no needs—-abnormally independent. Having needs was not safe. My family already barely made it by and to have a need that would offset the norm just wasn't even an option. And I am not just referencing materialistic needs—-this included nurturing, unconditional love, and connection.

I still remember as clear as day the summer going into my junior year in high school. As a cross-country and track runner, my shoe was torn at the toe; it had been worn for way more miles than its durability could withstand. I also worked full time at Bellevue's KFC for the summer. I was due for my paycheck and asked my mom if I could use some of my earnings for a new pair of shoes, since we were beginning training for the junior school year. I was met with, "Call your dad and ask him for it." I remember thinking *Huh?* It seemed so absurd to me knowing I was going to have several hundred dollars in a few days. But of course, it was expected in our house to sign our checks over to mom. And me needing one hundred dollars for a new pair of shoes would cut into what she planned on using the money for. I remember saying, "I don't want to call and ask him for more money—he already pays child support." After a back and forth with her dismissing what little my dad did pay, she said, "Go live with your father then." I remember her walking out of the bedroom and heading downstairs. My heart was racing; I was tearful, I was in shock, and all I could think to do in that moment was ask God. So, I said a mental prayer: *God, give me a sign if it is my time to go.*

I heard her coming back up the stairs. I was angry; I wanted to punch her. I was sad and felt disposable again. As she reached the top of the stairs, she threw sixty-nine dollars my way and told me I was not allowed to take any of my things, not even my violin, which had been my personal and sacred therapy since sixth grade. She turned around, walked out of the room, and went back downstairs. Couldn't have asked for more of a sign than that. OK, God, I hear you. I stood there in disbelief, still in shock I was getting kicked out because I needed new shoes I could buy with my own hard-earned money. *Can someone make this make sense?* I thought. *And what do I do next?* I pulled out the yellow pages, I called a cab, and that was it.

I can still see the look on my little brother David's face as the cab drove off. I remember my mom sitting on the living room couch while I waited for the cab. She blurted out, "You're leaving your brother? How is that going to make him feel?" She would use him as a hook, since I helped take care of him and tried to be the good big sister. I tried to protect him a lot, too, from what was going on in the home. We had a very strong bond and I considered us very close. So I believe she knew saying something like that would instill guilt in me. I think it was her ploy to get me to stay without her having to apologize for her behavior. I remember just ignoring her and all the comments she was spewing my way. There was never a correct response you could say to her without it being manipulated and coming back on you, so I kept my mouth shut. It was always best and safest not to speak. *Having needs is not safe* was an understatement.

In a cab with a strange man, I sat quietly in the backseat as we headed to Cleveland Hopkins Airport. As I was sniffling and replaying what had just occurred, the following thoughts ran through my mind...

I need to find a way to get to Illinois.

I have yet to speak to Dad. Does he even know I am coming?
I have flown alone before.
I will just walk to the Southwest ticket counter and let the
agent know what happened.
Maybe they will let me use their phone to call my dad.

This is where the mask of *having it all together* really started to show itself. I remember the wonderful woman at the ticket counter calling my stepmother, who had already been in communication with my mom. My father and stepmother purchased me a one-way ticket out of Ohio. After a few hours of waiting around the airport, just like that I was headed to my new home in Marengo, Illinois. Numbness had already settled in, but boarding the plane, I remember feeling so sad, like this was my fault. *Maybe bills were worse off than I knew and she really needed that hundred dollars?* I remember just staring out the window as we took off, uncertain what my life was about to look like. *Is my dad upset? Is he put off now having to feed another mouth? How will the extra expense affect their household? Is my stepmom upset about me disrupting their new family life?* The what-ifs that flooded my system were so much for my fifteen-year-old brain to understand and process. I couldn't help but to start tearing up. I didn't understand what I had done wrong. Why would my mom want to get rid of me because I wanted to use some of *my* money for a pair of tennis shoes? Is that how little I meant to her? A hundred dollars?

In the meantime the gentleman next to me asked, "Where are you headed?" I said, "To my dad's." He said, "Heading back from a visit?" I said, "No, moving in with him. My mom kicked me out." He said "_____." For years I had his exact words ingrained in my mind. They were incredibly hurtful. They were incredibly judgmental.

He alluded to me being kicked out because I was spoiled and not getting what I wanted. Those words stung for a long time and watered seeds of being *too much and too needy*.

I landed, and like always, my dad was standing there, ready to greet me with an awkward hug. I didn't know what to say. It was eerily quiet as we walked to the car. I had no belongings so there was no stop at baggage claim. We got into his car, and as we headed out of the chaos of traffic, he asked me, "So, what happened?" I remember feeling frozen because I didn't know what had been said to him and I didn't know who he would believe: me or my mom. I explained what happened and all he could say was, "I'm sorry." It was a long car ride home.

When I arrived at my dad's, it was so awkward. They went from having two full-time little kids to adding in a fifteen-year-old who had experienced nothing outside of trauma. I spent the rest of the summer acclimating to the new way of living, new rules, and new siblings, and gearing up for a new school as a junior in a small podunk cornfield of a town (Sorry, Marengo, tell me I am wrong.)

The coming years continued stacking the strength within. Missing my previous family while also trying to connect with my current family was difficult. Starting at a new school and trying to build friendships and relationships with people who had been going to school together since kindergarten was quite the feat. I lied every single day. To myself. To my parents. To my new acquaintances at school. I was constantly asked why on Earth I'd move to a small farm town full of cornfields and pastures. It was not like I could lead with, "My mom kicked me out." Then what? What opinion would they have of me? I hid so much of myself… the truth, the pain, the sadness, the loneliness. Man, I am so incredibly proud of that Candice. She took on so much at such a young age. The strength, while nothing to applaud, is quite impressive. And I say nothing to applaud simply because it was all unnecessary. A child shouldn't have to be strong for those reasons.

Strength turned out to be an integral part of my story, my way forward, my way of persevering when at times I wanted to give up. Watching my mom all those years be so strong and hyper-independent–through domestic violence, financial strain, so many kids with so much noise, bill collectors, police, and the court system–stamped that way of being as expected. She appeared unbothered when many things were occurring. She always worked multiple jobs, managed the home until we were old enough to help, took on chaos like she was the expert who created the word, and appeared like she had it all under control.

While I reflect and find many instances in my childhood and even adulthood where strength was a pillar I clung to, it is deeply saddening these circumstances even existed. While in adulthood, I take full credit for the fact that I played an active role in it, what I didn't realize was how my belief system was such a contributing factor. All these life experiences to which I was exposed allowed me to subconsciously water seeds of belief about myself that would set the tone and foundation for many years to come.

It was not safe to be me. Constantly berated, judged, criticized. *Candice, you're too this, you're too that*—it was like a record that played on repeat in my head. I began to show up as a Candice who would just laugh at it all.

I wore the mask of happy, outgoing, fun Candice.

I paraded the persona of, "I don't hurt, it doesn't bother me, that's their problem."

I began to believe it all myself as a way to cope and make it through each day.

Over the years, I even convinced social workers and police officers after multiple CPS calls and reports that all was well.

This became a way of living and even followed me to my father's. My summer visits to his house revealed laughter, a nice big house, pizza every Friday, lots of kids in a safe neighborhood, water and electricity that stayed on, no bugs... it all seemed like a dream. But living with him year-round was an adjustment. I started seeing beyond what my short visits revealed. And I learned quickly that this was just another home reinforcing that it was not safe to be me.

My dad would drink and get emotional some nights. Some nights he was just utterly disgusted... at what, I didn't know. It almost felt like clockwork, but you never knew which nights he would explode; it really was a toss of the dice. I remember one night we got on the topic of hair, since I had an appointment the next day. He had asked what I planned to do with it and when I responded that I was getting a few highlights, he said, "You say what you see is what you get, but that's bullshit. If that was the case you wouldn't color your hair, get fake nails, go to the tanning bed. YOU'RE FAKE." And then it would erupt. We would go back and forth arguing because I was not going to remain quiet. My stepmom certainly didn't say anything to stick up for me. She looked more annoyed than anything. Eventually he would run me down into the ground enough with cruel, hurtful words—"You're a fat fuck, you're a beached whale, you're going to turn out just like your mom"---that I would walk right out the front door and down Blackhawk Lane until I felt he would be passed out and it would be safe to come back in.

It wasn't safe to have an opinion.

It wasn't safe to ask questions.

It wasn't safe to disagree.

It wasn't safe to be visible.

To some degree it wasn't even safe to laugh.

Knowing what I know now and the many masks I wore, he triggered me. I was in fact fake, but not for the reasons he claimed. I bottled myself up and withdrew so much that I felt completely alone. I knew this feeling but it felt even deeper. Feeling judged by siblings and a mother with whom I lived my whole life is one thing; receiving it from a father I recently moved in with hit differently. I once heard, "Daughters learn to love by the love they receive from their fathers," and I can never unhear that. My father's love, action (or inaction), and behaviors set the foundation of the love I would feel I deserved in life.

Since retiring, I have spent time discovering the masks I wear to feel safe, and slowly, as I remove them I notice... *I am still safe*. The work I have done all these years is allowing me to welcome myself home. To unfold like flower petals in bloom. I take comfort in knowing there is so much more left of me to discover, and for the first time in my life, it feels safe to do so. I get so excited to discover what is still beneath. Beneath the masks that are starting to become unglued. Beneath the remnants of fear and vulnerability. Beneath the conditioning that has been slowly unraveling. She's there. She's me. She is also you. Waiting to emerge like the flower petal on a warm sunny day. Be in the excitement to see you, to meet you. Another season, another version of self is revealed. Reader, if you also relate to the need to wear masks to feel safe in your surroundings, I witness you.

PERMISSION GRANTED to peel back the layers and reveal the authentic you.

The Fairytale Era

*"I'm just a girl, standing in front of a boy,
asking him to love her."*

—Anna Scott

I found myself feeling alone much of my high school experience. Just another way I continued watering the seeds of *not being enough* and *being unlovable*. I was single and okay with it. Sure, I wanted a connection and to have dates for homecoming and prom, but my friends were great, too. I think my entire junior year was about adjusting to the location, the school, and new relationships.

The summer came, and I was working at Taco Bell. I saved so much of my money because I was pretty frugal given how I grew up. I knew what it was like to be without, so I was comfortable there. I didn't feel I needed much. Knowing what I know now, I also did not feel worthy of having good or nice things. I saved as much as I could but also was adamant about paying for my own car insurance, cell phone bill, and outings with friends.

Going into senior year, I was excited! It was senior year—what every teenager looked forward to. It was football and homecoming season, fresh crisp air with the smell of apple cider, colorful leaves falling to the ground; it was my favorite time of year. I remember feeling a little more settled and found myself coming out of my shell. I attended football games, homecoming with girlfriends, and even had some of my best run times in cross country. I had one of the lead roles in our school's musical and felt like I was thriving.

The middle of my senior year, though, everything shifted. *I met a boy.* He was the cutest, goofiest, charming, and although he couldn't manage to get to class on time and do his work, and did the most outrageous things to get a laugh, I was fond of him. To be honest, I had no clue who he was at first. It is a funny story in and of itself how I even discovered this boy. I used my extra class period supporting the secretary in the main office. I would go around and collect attendance slips from all the doors, and he was always on the slip as either "not present" or "tardy." I thought, *Who is this Mike guy? Why can't he ever get to school on time? What a schmuck!* Hahahaha, joke was on me; little did I know we would marry one day.

It turned out we had a few mutual friends, and the more that I saw him around, the more my crush on him grew. Eventually, I got his number from a friend of mine in study hall. My friend Erin and I called and his mother answered. She told us he was out working on his car. Hours later, we called back and she said the same thing. We called the entire day; his mother must have been so annoyed.

Even more cringey than calling all day, Erin and I were out on the town on a Friday evening and decided to head to his house. As we pulled into his driveway, the snow was falling pretty hard and–this would be my luck–we got stuck in his driveway. Mike came outside to greet us. His driveway was so long, and Erin and I were just sitting there laughing hysterically until tears streamed down our faces. Oh my gosh, those were some of the best times. I am in full gratitude sharing this cringey but funny moment with you all. Life in that moment was not so serious. It felt like I was actually a teenager. I was met with laughter, happiness, joyfulness, and spontaneity, something I didn't get to experience much of at all. I guess you could say I was *in my essence*. I was also met with a boy who was super cute in his corduroy pants, blonde highlighted tips, and Shaggy-like appearance (seriously—he had that nickname at school because he resembled Shaggy from *Scooby Doo)*.

Once the initial awkwardness waned, Mike, Erin, and I went into his house where I met his mom, dad, sister, and niece. I can't even imagine the thoughts going through their heads. We went into his room, where I immediately noticed his black lights, Ozzy Osbourne music playing, and what smelled like Cool Water cologne. I took this all in while he quickly moved his dirty laundry from the floor to his closet.

We hung out and had a great time. Fun conversations that included awkward pauses figuring out what to say next, which typically triggered an awkward laugh from Erin, who was sitting with us witnessing the entire thing unfold. We laughed at our teeth and how whitish-yellow they looked with his black light on. Man, let us go back in time for a moment. The feeling of wonder, excitement, butterflies, all tucked alongside nervousness. *Does he like me? Am I being weird? Oh no, I just said that out loud! He's so sweet. He's really smart. I think he likes me.*

I eventually moved past the cringey, clingy stage and we were inseparable—I know I seem to contradict myself in that statement, but I think it is because it was two-sided. We loved hanging out with each other. We both filled each other up in ways we needed at that time in our lives. Every Friday we went to Wendy's for our dinner date followed by a movie. I had Goobers and a Coke every time! He was a gentleman and paid each week with money he earned cleaning his dad's big semi-truck and helping with the cows. We built a love quickly. He was my everything, and I believed I was his. We spent the rest of the year hanging out and being in the self-discovery and curiosity of the relationship and its future.

My dad, however, was not a fan of Mike. One night, I was a few minutes late and he was waiting up—inebriated, of course. As soon as I walked in I could feel the energy in the room and knew it wasn't going to be good. Still a virgin, I could nonetheless feel my father's judgment and the assumptions. But I also knew there was no convincing him otherwise, so I didn't say a word. My body was stiff, I could feel my heart beat into my throat, and I got hot and clammy. So, I did what felt safest: I lied. I told him I was pulled over by an unmarked car and that was what led to my tardiness. Just by the look on my dad's face I knew I'd come up with the dumbest lie ever.

The next day they contacted the police department informing them of my story and through some varying exchanges, now even more fearful to come clean, I was being booked for falsifying a police report. My stepmom escorted me to the police department to turn myself in. I remember standing there to get fingerprinted, thinking to myself how deep down I was just a few minutes late. *How has this escalated to here? How am I getting arrested for this?* I understood the dishonesty and the lesson I was to learn. But to me, it was much deeper.

Standing there for the mugshot holding back tears, I felt so misunderstood. Kicked out of my mom's for asking a clarifying question, now arrested at my dad's because I felt scared to speak my truth. This watered the seed planted years earlier, *I am a bad person.*

After court proceedings I ended up with several hours of community service, hefty fines, and probation for a year. Pending no issues, this would later be erased from my record. It was a humiliating process and a lesson learned. That was the beginning of the end. My lying really jeopardized my relationship with my dad and stepmom. I could feel the questioning, judgment, and disbelief everytime I spoke. And I was harboring anger because never once did they ask why I lied. They just handed out punishments and judgment and never thought to consider why it felt safer to lie than come forward in honesty.

A few months later, graduation season had arrived! I felt like I was finally a legal adult, even though I was seventeen and felt like I had been adulting for years. I was so happy to be celebrated by all my family and friends. Those who came to celebrate me were so generous with their words, their prayers, their gifts. I was even awarded a small scholarship, which I was proud to receive. It was the deep breath I needed and a permission slip to myself, saying I was on my own.

Also during this time, my dad dished out lots of ultimatums regarding my life and relationships, and used things like paying for college, my cell phone, and my car as a way to manipulate me into doing what he wanted. He liked having control, and as a newly graduated teen in her fairytale era, I didn't like being controlled. No longer scared of him, I was ready to stand up to him, to speak my truth. We got into a huge argument where I vividly remember telling him to take it all. That I didn't need those things and could do without. I felt empowered. I felt finally free to say what I wished without fear of his words. I no longer respected him as my father—deep down I knew he was just another version of someone else I knew all too well, just with a different addiction.

A few days after graduation, I headed to the ATM machine to pull out money and received a receipt stating *insufficient funds*. Now I knew I had money—I had recently deposited all my graduation money from family and friends, and I worked full time at the local nursing home. At the time, I had four figures. But my money was gone. All of it. GONE. I was furious. I panicked. This was what I was supposed to survive on. I ran into the bank and stood in line waiting for a bank teller to assist me. It felt like the longest few minutes ever. In my mind, I was retracing my steps from the prior day to make sure I did in fact deposit all the money. Recalling the exchange in the drive-thru bank window. Visualizing the bank receipt I had that showed my balance just under four thousand dollars. As my heart raced and my mouth went dry, I continued asking myself, *What am I going to do?* It was my turn. I ran up to the counter.

"Hi, I received a receipt at the ATM that stated insufficient funds," I said to the teller. "I just deposited over twenty-five hundred dollars a few days ago—I am so confused where it is."

After some research it was disclosed to me that twenty-five hundred dollars had been withdrawn by my stepmom, and the remaining balance I had went toward pending transactions. Being underage when I opened my account, I had to have an adult as a joint member, so that explained the access to the account. It was a legal route for my father and stepmother to keep me under their thumb. They wanted control, to feel power over me.

No phone to communicate—stripping me of my voice. No vehicle to drive back and forth to community college and my full-time job. No money for basic needs. They sure put me in a position to make me feel like I had no other choice but to stay. At seventeen years old, I packed my belongings and left. Once again feeling discarded by my parents–because of their *my way or else mentality*, their need to control, and their theft of my money–my seeds of *too much, unlovable,* and *I am a bad person* continued to be watered.

I moved in with Mike, and his parents were kind enough to give me a bedroom upstairs, so I was able to have privacy with boundaries. Because I was under eighteen and had no money to put down on a car, Mike's father decided to cosign on an older car for me —-something that would get me where I needed to go without breaking the bank. I can recall sitting at their kitchen table in their house on Root Road, feeling so sad but showing only strength, listening to Mike's father ramble on about my dad, trying to make me feel better. This man was telling me how great of a kid I was, but deep down, all I could feel was *not enough*. It felt like I kept failing and disappointing everyone. Why couldn't I see what this ex-Marine and Vietnam War Veteran was telling me? *Why could I only see failure? Lies. Bad.* When he offered to cosign for a vehicle, I did not know how to receive it. I was in a predicament where I had no choice, so it felt extremely uncomfortable but I accepted. He took me to Fred, a car salesman Mike's family went to for their purchases, and they both helped me pick out something reliable and affordable. Someone who has known me less than a year was not only taking me into his home to live rent-free, but also cosigning on a vehicle for me. I remember driving off in such gratitude, thanking God for Mike's parents who had shown up out of thin air.

The year flew by as I attended community college and worked full time. Mike graduated high school, and we were set to move into our first apartment together. We were so excited to share this space and make it ours. With my car now on its last leg, I decided to go to a dealership to look for something newer that would be more safe and reliable through the heavy Midwestern winters. I found a car I loved and decided to purchase it. The salesman I was working with came back to tell me I had gotten denied, since my credit was poor. I explained to him I didn't understand how my credit would be poor; if anything, I didn't have any credit. He shared with me that I had been sent to collections for an unpaid bill. I discovered that once my mother had kicked me out, she had put a landline in my name and run up the bill until they disconnected it. They sent me to collections for nonpayment, tanking my credit score.

At that moment, I felt so defeated. *How does a mother ruin their child in so many different ways? I am no longer there and she is still wrecking my life,* I thought to myself. I managed to keep it together while I was at the car dealership and then cried all the way home. *Why does everything have to be so hard, God? Why can't I get a break?* Knowing my dad had purchased brand new cars for my brother and sister, I felt cheated. I felt things were so unfair. At eighteen years of age, I was pressing charges against my mom in order to get my credit cleared.

Months later, I came home from working the nightshift and fell asleep on the couch. I remember Mike walking in through the front door unexpectedly. I was still half asleep, but he placed his SpongeBob SquarePants lunch box on the living room floor and told me to empty it as he walked off and went to the bathroom. I got up and grabbed his lunch box, and he came out of the bathroom, meeting me in our mini-kitchen. As I opened the lunchbox, inside it was a small box. I remember having the biggest smile on my face despite my sleepiness. As I opened it, I saw it was an engagement ring. He stood there all dressed up for work and proposed to me. I was so giddy and excited, and also felt so loved and cared for. I finally really mattered to someone. Someone loved all parts of me unconditionally. *Someone wanted me. Someone picked me. Someone chose me.*

We continued living our lives, going to movies and Wendy's on Friday nights, and his parents' house on Sundays so he could wash the big semi and I could lay in his mom's bed and watch rom-coms all day. We had a pretty solid routine. I was still working at the nursing home; however, I found myself working doubles a lot because for some reason, Mike struggled to keep his jobs. I started getting so frustrated and resentful–I was working sixteen-hour long days, and I would come home to him laying on the couch watching cartoons with no plans of job searching. I started to wonder if this was what my life was going to look like: married to a k-dult (kid adult) while I worked to make sure all the bills could be paid. I started questioning what our future would look like.

It was the Christmas holiday season, my second favorite time of the year. Snow twinkled in the yards, ice covered the bare tree branches, the smell of nutmeg, cinnamon, and cocoa filled stores and homes. Christmas music played in the grocery store as I rushed around to fill the cart with ingredients for holiday treats in preparation of Mike's family coming into town. Jen, his older sister, came by our place and hung out with us over dinner and a movie. We started talking, which led us down the path of the military. She shared so much information, I thought, *Man, this sounds too good to be true. Full-time pay, medical and dental benefits, college tuition, housing allowance, opportunity for raises, all while being in a position to serve others... well, that is a full "heck yes"!* I needed to know more.

I spoke to Mike about my desire to join the military. I felt in a rut and needed to branch out and do something that would not only be fulfilling but bring me joy, purpose, and job security. I was watching all the middle-aged women at my job, and they struggled so much with back pain and other ailments due to lifting and transitioning the residents. I wanted more in life. I wanted to be a nurse!

I started my process and took my Armed Services Vocational Aptitude Battery (ASVAB), the military's entrance test. I scored high enough to qualify for the Hospital Corpsman rate, which is what I desired since I lacked a nursing degree. I remember driving all the way to Ohio at the last minute to retrieve my birth certificate, which was the last piece of information they needed to process my application. I called my dad and asked if I could come to his house, as I had something I needed to tell him. I arrived, I sat down in the chair I used to always sit in, and shared the big news. The relief *and* excitement he and my stepmom had for me was so surprising.

It came time to tell Mike the news. We had already spoken at length about it, but now it was official. It wasn't that I didn't *want* to be with him; I just struggled with the vision of what our life together would look like because he lacked the level of motivation and maturity I was looking for. When I shared the news with him, I could see his fear, his sadness, all his emotions. He understood but didn't want us to be apart. So he also joined. We both left the same day to bootcamp. Sitting in a room, just him and I alone as we were waiting for the other recruits to arrive, neither of us knew what to expect. It had been just a matter of a few weeks from the decision, to the execution, to the government now owning us.

Reader, fairy tales had me excited about growing up and getting married.

Handsome charming boy comes in and rescues a girl, sweeping her off her feet. They live happily ever after. The end! Growing up in a single-parent home, I never really got to experience or witness a marriage. Because of this, I held onto the love stories I saw in fairytales as a glimpse into what I hoped relationships would look and feel like. Mike arrived just in time. Just like in the movies, he came in and rescued me, from the dysfunction and emotional turmoil I was experiencing as the child of an alcoholic and an addict. He was exactly who I needed, my own Prince Charming. Looking back, I realized I was looking for someone to save me. To rescue me and make me feel valued, loved, and accepted, when in reality no one can do that but me. Reader, I'm not sure if you can relate to my fairytale era, but if so, know that you get to create your own fairytales, but you must start first within yourself.

PERMISSION GRANTED to honor your intuition and trust your inner wisdom.

The Deployment Era

"The only way to deal with an unfree world is to become so absolutely free that your very existence is an act of rebellion."

—Albert Camus

Bootcamp wasn't difficult for me. This is where I thrived because of the way I grew up. Rules—check. Chores—check. Listen—check. Don't talk back—check. Broken sleep—check. Watch over everyone—check. My biggest struggle with bootcamp was the sit ups. I'd had surgery to diagnose my endometriosis and the post-surgery recovery had really affected my stomach muscles. But we did so much physical fitness–marching, walking, running–that the weight I had gained after high school and surgery just melted off.

On graduation day, I felt such a sense of pride. I had worked so hard physically, which was my own personal challenge. I looked and felt the best I had ever felt in my entire life. I felt strong. I felt confident. I felt successful. I was looking forward to what was next.

Mike and I got to go back to our hometown to hang out for the weekend right after graduation. We had a lot of fun telling each other bootcamp stories, joking about our Recruit Division Commanders (RDCs), the rules, the food, the late night roving watches. It was nice to reconnect and feel like we achieved this big milestone together. It led me to the thought that *everything happens for a reason...* maybe the purpose and lesson in his reluctance to get a steady job was so I would join the military. *To start a career,* I told myself. Following that weekend, we spent a few months apart to attend specialty training for the jobs we would be assigned while serving. During that few-month gap, he flew in so we could go to the courthouse and get married.

We arrived at the courthouse. I wore a knee-high white dress that I picked out at some random store at the mall, clogged shoes, earrings, and my hair spiked as high as it would go. (I wanted to feel as feminine as possible since the navy cut it off in bootcamp.) I had a ginormous knot in my stomach. My throat felt tight. I felt judgment from parents and others in attendance. I fought myself on whether this was my intuition screaming, *STOP, DON'T DO IT,* urging me to call off the wedding and enjoy being young. To slow down. I convinced myself that my fears were no longer valid, that he had a job now. I no longer had to worry about the concerns I had before. So, I decided the little voice was fear... cold feet... I silenced it and kept it moving. Him eighteen, me nineteen, we were husband and wife.

He left the next day and flew back to Florida, where he finished a couple more weeks of his training before heading to our first duty station. Because we were now married, I was able to get orders to the same vicinity and reported just a little bit later. I remember not being there long before he took off on his first deployment in November. I focused on my work with the determination to be a great asset to the service. I worked twelve-hour rotations on a neurology unit, and it felt like the six months flew by. My off days were spent hanging with new friends and anxiously awaiting news from Mike, who called less and less as time went on.

Rumors of cheating swirled on both our ends. He was very flirtatious and friendly and never called me, and I hung out with a husband and wife who both had male names. I didn't think anything of it at the time but, when I would send Mike emails disclosing my plans and giving him the details, I should have said they were a heterosexual married couple. I also discovered my love for dancing. I went to girls' college nights and danced on bars by myself; I even got body piercings in questionable places. Although normal behaviors for my age, I could see how these would raise huge red flags for a spouse. I was what some would call *naive*. As exposed as I had been to life growing up, I suppose in other ways I had been extremely sheltered. My behavior drove him into being distant because he didn't really know what to say. We struggled to connect and communicate, while each of us was also trying to adjust to military life at nineteen and twenty.

He returned from deployment, and it felt a little off for a bit. We both had to get to know one another again. The military has a palpable way of making you grow up! I enrolled in classes, as I had a strong desire to pursue my nursing career. As I worked in the medical field, connected deeply and passionately with my patients, and gained the trust of the varying officers alongside whom I worked, my confidence started to build: this was something I was capable of achieving.

Fall was here, and I began noticing some things that felt off in my body. Sitting in class I had the biggest pain in my pubic region. I wasn't exactly sure what it was, but it sure did take my breath away. Over the course of the next couple weeks, things didn't improve, so I took a pregnancy test. I sat on the bathroom toilet in our cozy apartment first thing in the morning and to my surprise, I was pregnant. *WHAT?!* And "yay!" all at the same time. I remember being so excited. My entire body lit up. After two surgical interventions, cauterization of endometriosis patches, and multiple cyst removals, I had been told that my odds were higher than before, but I hadn't expected a pregnancy this soon. I took a total of three tests to make sure I really saw *two lines.* The next weeks were filled with the energy and thoughts of, *Holy cow, I am going to be a mother,* and *Oh, my god, I am going to be a mother.* I immediately shifted.

Months flew by and we had a daughter. Shortly after Natalya Mrie was born, Mike started his workups preparing him for his second deployment. The day I went back to work, he left for his six-week cruise and after that another six-month haul. It was a lot to process, him leaving not only me for six months, but our baby, too. And let's not forget about my hormones trying to get back to normal while also breastfeeding and pumping around the clock. I had to figure out how to add twelve-hour shifts and alternating long weekends to the mix. I spent all my time with Nattie when not at work. We spent time together with my friend, Katie, who had also just had a baby. We both joked about how Nattie and Katie's baby would grow up together and someday get married, since we were such besties. They even got pictures together for Valentine's Day.

Outside of Katie and a couple of my aunts, Marilyn and Joyce, who lived fairly close, it was me and my sidekick, Nattie. I was very disciplined, some days going to bed at 4 p.m. because I had to wake up so early for shift work, coupled with morning tasks such as nursing, pumping, feeding, and getting all my stuff together. Like most new moms, I was a zombie.

I spent that deployment just enjoying motherhood, working, acknowledging how I was changing, and taking online college classes toward my desired nursing degree. I was also studying my craft working toward advancing in rank, which led to late nights, slower responses to Mike, and study sessions with male friends. All of this led Mike to grow suspicious that I was cheating.

I was so excited when the deployment was over and we could all be a whole family again. But, things were different this time. He came home a different person. He was distant, he was avoidant, he was angry, and he lied about everything. I didn't know what had happened to my husband and I certainly didn't recognize him. I learned only recently what happened in this traumatic time in his life, when he shared it with me.

As he transitioned back into a work schedule, things continued to seem off. I asked questions, tried to understand, but each time he would just shut down. I could see something was wrong. My gut was telling me there was someone else. But, was it my gut or was it jumping to conclusions? I was doing his laundry and finding phone numbers written on torn pieces of paper. I would call to talk to him at work and coworkers in his shop would say he wasn't working. Late night accidental butt dials as he talked to other women, consoling them. He forgot our anniversary. I felt like this was the beginning of the end.

September arrived, and we were surprised by a pregnancy. I was happy for Nattie to have a sibling, but I was met with feelings of confusion regarding the status of Mike and I. Everything lined up to show me he couldn't even take on the responsibility of one child, let alone two. It was not a question as to whether I was going to go through with it; I was just aware that even though I wasn't a single mom, I would likely act in that role. Mike was having outbursts of rage, punching holes in the walls. He was at a level beyond what I was comfortable with. One night, he even picked up our oversized side chair and slammed it down. In that moment, I felt so triggered as it took me back to childhood scenes where the same things happened. I froze. I felt my upper body stiff and locked. Wanting to move but unable to. Jeremy, our roommate, came in from the garage after hearing all the commotion, grabbing Mike and telling him that he needed to leave.

Not too long after, he went to stay with his friends. We were not separated but he needed space. Both of us had a lot of underlying trust issues and it was not healthy for us to be around one another at the time. I still had Jeremy and his girlfriend around a lot and my days were consumed with Nattie, work, and pregnancy. I felt so alone. I felt so confused. I felt so bad for bringing another child into this situation. I found myself visiting the chaplain, who I saw often on the unit I worked, and found him comforting to talk to. I shared with him where I had messed up, how things had been perceived through both deployments. I also shared how Mike was so different and how he was so angry and hurtful toward me.

Now in mid-October, I had an OB appointment. I was so excited to see the baby, hear the heartbeat, and be in full excitement of what was to come. I needed it with all that was going on. I remember like it was yesterday! Cold room, long ultrasound wand, the black and white image on the screen, *and his face*. The OB's face as he looked for the heartbeat. He then motioned to the corpsman to get another provider. Being so familiar with this work I knew what was happening. My heart sank. I felt like I was being smothered, unable to catch my breath. My stomach had a knot, one that made me want to vomit. I laid there feeling like I was in a tunnel. I had my friend Shannon with me because Mike didn't show up to the appointment. In that moment it was confirmed—there was no heartbeat and the pregnancy was no longer viable. I lost it. I cried out all my sorrow. The loss of the baby, Mike not being there, Mike being different and no longer my Prince Charming. I felt like all the air had been knocked out of me. I blamed myself for taking cold medicine. I blamed myself for arguing and being stressed out. I blamed myself for killing my baby. "It was my fault," I said out loud. "My one job in this world is to have and protect my kids, and I failed."

I was frozen. I was numb. I was mad. Before leaving I had to schedule a dilation and curettage (D&C), a surgical procedure to clean out my uterus. With a flat affect, I drove home, reminding myself I needed to suck it up because I had a daughter to tend to. I could not be swimming in the shit because she needed me. This occurred right before Halloween weekend, so I spent the entire weekend into the next miscarrying all by myself while pretending all was well so Nattie could enjoy herself. I grieved, cramped, bled, cried, worked, repeat.

The day of surgery arrived, and I went alone. Mike never showed up, never called, I never heard from him. Wheeled back to the OR, I slid onto the bed from the gurney, stared at the bright lights as they placed the mask on my face, and started counting backwards. I drifted off into the in-between. As I was waking up, shouting, "Give me my baby back, give me my baby back" while kicking those near me, all I could hear were little babies crying in the recovery room with other moms who had just had cesarean sections. I was devastated. *Where was mine? I want my baby.* I felt so alone. I felt like such a fool as I heard my dad's voice say so clearly and loudly, "I told you so."

Though distraught I focused on my recovery while taking care of the house, watching Nattie, and working full time. I was presented with an opportunity to attend advanced training in California for three months just after New Year's. This would provide me with a certification that would transfer into the civilian sector should I decide a long-term career in the service wasn't for me. I had a conversation with Mike about it, because he would have to take on the responsibility of Nattie. After a lengthy discussion, we both decided we could make this work and both our commands were going to support us. I was to leave January 1st, which was just a month away.

We navigated the holidays, making it special for Nattie, and then before we knew it, it was January 1st. I remember loading up my car and driving off with tears streaming down my face. I could barely see in front of me. I had never been away from my Nattie outside of work. She was my sidekick, and I didn't know how I was going to navigate three months without her little mullet head singing and dancing to *Dora The Explorer*. I also worried about how Mike was going to manage it all, since he had not been that involved with her and was typically the one deployed.

The drive was so therapeutic. The clouds, sunshine, and, as I drove further west, the warmth. As I made my way from coast to coast, I reminded myself why I was doing this. I arrived in California on January 4th. It was so peaceful.

The smell of the ocean, the dark sky lit up by the brightness of the stars, the palm trees… it was beautiful. As I laid down for bed, I reflected on the past four days… driving, processing, imagining, hoping, feeling, all the ebbs and flows of leaving your family for the first time. I can't speak for men, but as a woman and mother, it felt like an emptiness I couldn't quite describe. Even though what I was doing was going to advance our little family, I still felt a sense of guilt for leaving her. I knew what it felt like to be left—-*What if she didn't understand?* I had to trust that she was safe and sound in Mike's care. I had to surrender control, and for me, control was what offered me a sense of safety. By controlling a situation, I knew what to expect.

January 29th is a day I will never forget. I called Nattie like I usually do every morning, but this time the call went very differently. My sitter asked me when Mike would be coming to get Nattie. I explained to her he usually gets off around five and should be coming at the normal time. That was when she revealed that he had not been back. Not understanding what she meant and asking her to clarify, she told me he had dropped Nattie off on January 4th and had not been back to get her. She stated she was only sharing this with me because she was out of food and diapers and he wasn't returning her phone calls.

Tunnel vision.

Ringing in the ears.

Heart erupting through my mouth.

Nausea.

I stood there frozen.

I couldn't speak.

I couldn't process it.

My worst nightmare was coming true—not being able to protect my daughter. Feeling helpless. Feeling immense mom guilt, telling myself I should have never left. *I should have known better*, I told myself. *How could I have been so dumb? My poor Nattiebug. How awful she must feel. How scared she must be.* Lots of shame set in. *I still have two more months,* I told myself. I reported what was happening to my superiors but was told that since my daughter was safe and being taken care of, it might just be best to let it play out. That these things happen all the time. I couldn't wrap my head around that. I felt so helpless. *How was this alright?* Doing the only thing I could from there, I increased my phone calls to Nattie. Every break I got I attempted to call and talk to her. Sometimes I got lucky, other times she was napping or playing with other kids. The sitter was reassuring me every step of the way, making me feel as at peace as one could expect given the circumstances.

When I was finally able to reach Mike to ask what in the world was going on, he attempted to deny it all. Everything he said was a lie. I broke. With parents involved in substance abuse, I'd always steered away. I was a good girl. I followed the rules. I would never be like them. Never had a desire to drink, smoke, or do any recreational drugs. Never had a desire to cheat. When this all erupted, I caved on it all. I went to the bar with friends and got so piss drunk, I did unforgivable things that a married person should not do. Everything I had been compartmentalizing over the years reared its head.

Feeling like my family discarded me.

Joining and transitioning into the military.

My daughter needing me and I wasn't there.

I still had a belief that I killed my baby.

Going through my miscarriage alone.

Surgery and recovery alone.

Marriage falling apart with violence, avoidance, and lies.

… And now my abandoned daughter.

Little Candice was triggered. I knew what it felt like to be discarded and tossed aside. To not be a priority. I couldn't imagine my daughter also having to feel this pain. It swallowed me up daily. However, knowing what I know now, the reality of that being the truth wasn't likely. She was surrounded by a loving sitter and little friends all day, but my inner child couldn't see that. The pain I was projecting onto the situation kept me in shackles, limiting my movement forward.

On top of all that I was experiencing and feeling, I added more shame. Shame for my actions in the midst of sudden pain, chaos, and confusion. I couldn't keep it in. I decided it was time to face reality. Nervous and scared, I picked up my cell phone and called Mike. Angry, hurt, trying to understand it all–even the things from before I left–I informed him that I had cheated on him. He told me he had to pull over because he was driving. His voice quivered, he shared his sudden nausea, he cried. I felt awful, felt shame, felt embarrassed, and I also felt like there was no way I would ever be able to forgive him for abandoning our daughter, no matter his reasoning. He didn't ask questions, I didn't ask questions, and that was the end of our fairy tale love.

I often look back on this relationship and see two very young kids that truly loved one another. I feel we got married out of fear of losing one another. Feeling connection and a deep love, we were a means to fill each other's cups, which constantly felt empty otherwise. We had so much love for one another, and though his actions were less than desirable, mine were no better or worse. They all just were. In one of my mindset card decks, Just PIVOT, I have a card that is focused on blame. It reads: *Shifting blame is easy. It takes grit and courage to own your part in the story.* So here I am, owning my part in the story. My part in our dissolution. I take ownership for my actions, which led to a love that fell apart. Whether we could have rebuilt our love, who knows. But my personal self-sabotage ended up being the nail in the coffin.

Mistakes are a way to learn and grow, if we actually learn and grow from them. Mike and I both made many mistakes in our season together. But, Natalya was not one of those mistakes. She has the very best of both of us. The little thing she does with her tongue when she talks, her open-mindedness, and her deep intellect she gets from him. Her drive, motivation, and sensitivity she gets from me. She is incredible. Perfect. And I am forever grateful for him to have brought me such a gift.

Though this chapter is filled with a depth of pain, regret, and real-life, self-soothing coping mechanisms, there is also a behind-the-scenes that would not unfold until many years later. Mike suffered some immense trauma while serving that he had not come to terms with, leading to his thoughts, actions, and behaviors during this period. I'm not giving him a permission slip or pass, but we must always make an effort to meet each other with an attempt to understand, to listen, to offer grace and compassion when it is warranted.

Know that the way someone treats you is a deep reflection of how they feel about themselves.

PERMISSION GRANTED to learn, grow, and evolve with each experience.

The Resilience Era

"Whatever is in me is stronger than
what is out there to defeat me."

—Caroline Myss

It was a hard morning dropping Nattie off at the sitter's knowing I had just been away for a few months. I felt some sadness knowing I was already back to work, as well as some apprehensiveness checking into the new command. I typically liked to remain under the radar, but in my case— legal separation, single mother, a new home, a new daycare, and a new specialty—I knew I was potentially going to have to share all of this with leadership to keep them informed. *Deep breath, inhale, exhale, you've got this, Candice!*

I set the goal for this duty station to get picked up for a Medical Enlisted Commissioning Program (MECP) that would allow me to spend three years as a college student while still serving as active duty. This was going to offer us a sense of financial safety and job security, while also fulfilling my deep desire of becoming a nurse. Laser focused, I spent my days dedicated to that vision. Mike, unfortunately, was not reliable, but thankfully I had an amazing network of friends who dropped everything just to help me.

My friends and I were a military generation spent at war: Ramadi, Fallujah, Iraq, Afghanistan, and Guantanamo

Bay to name a few. During my training after bootcamp, the bombing of the USS Cole occurred, and shortly thereafter the events of 9/11 unfolded. War was all we knew—the constant movement, deployments, training, and combat. Unfortunately many of my friends spent multiple long tours in these locations. They came home different. There were some who didn't return. Those who did, suffered silently. Many learned to self-soothe with alcohol, smoking, food, and prescription drug abuse. There seemed to be such a stigma attached to mental health support.

While my focus was to dive into school and have command involvement to build a strong and competitive package, I was also met with new life experiences that would force me to hold myself together through it all, once again. So many events in my two years at this command impacted me in ways I can't ever forget. In my short stint there, I was drugged, physically assaulted, and raped. Three separate events. Three different men. Three different trips to hell.

It was a holiday weekend and I was at an apartment complex where many of my coworkers lived. We were all laughing, joking around, and telling the most inappropriate, foul jokes. Music was playing; I even recall my friend Steven being the jokester he was and dancing awfully to gain laughs from the ladies in the room. From there, I have no memory.

The next morning, I woke up not feeling great. Puzzled, I only remembered consuming one glass of red wine the entire night. I didn't understand why I felt so different—almost like a fuzziness, a haze. I checked in with everyone and shared how I didn't feel well. A couple friends started laughing. I stood there confused—their body language told me something was wrong. That's when Steven said he and Antwon had placed two Ambien pills in my glass of wine the night before. "We wanted to see how you would act!" he said with laughter as he shifted his body to the others in the room. Immediately mortified, not knowing how I acted or the things I said, I dismissed my feelings of anger and betrayal and joined the room in laughter. *I need these friends,* I told myself. *They are what is keeping me from being alone and feeling the shame of my self-inflicted circumstances.*

I sat there listening to everyone play out the night, sharing how I acted, repeating the things I said. I was humiliated. Apparently, I was quite the entertainer... my actions and behaviors, though I remembered none of them, had kept everyone on their toes.

When I left, I was immediately flooded with thoughts: if we had a urinalysis, I would pop up positive. I didn't want to report what had happened because I felt bad for my friends. This was a theme in my life, constantly making excuses for others' poor behaviors even if they negatively impacted me. I remember leaving and feeling sad that I had been used at the expense of some laughter. They hadn't even considered the ramifications of their actions. With friends like that, who needs friends?

Friday evenings were my one night a week to unwind. I typically hung out at my place with my favorite sitter, after Nattie was all tucked away in bed. This particular evening, my friend April and I met up with coworkers at the local pub for happy hour. We arrived and it was a full house. So many from the clinic were there. It was karaoke night so lots of singing was happening. "Sweet Caroline" and Journey songs filled the bar, along with dancing and storytelling.

I had just finished my second beer when April approached me wanting to leave because she had a sudden headache. I was actually having a good time and didn't want to leave yet, but I needed a ride home. A coworker, Chase, overheard and nonchalantly said, "You live right down the road from me, I can drop you off." Married, with a kid at home, he seemed trustworthy enough. I said, "Oh, awesome, thanks." As the night wrapped up, I finished my third Michelob Ultra, nibbled on the rest of my appetizers, then hopped in the car with Chase.

Time warped. Suddenly I was in a kitchen standing over a sink, barely able to stand, throwing up. Everything was fuzzy and blurry. Time stopped. I woke up in an unfamiliar bed. So confused, wiping my eyes while looking up at the ceiling, I noticed I was naked. As I sat up in a hurry to grab my clothes, I noticed a little boy standing next to me staring into my eyes. I gasped in shock. I didn't know where I was. *Who was this boy looking at me? Where am I?* I looked to my left to see Chase sound asleep. I saw my clothes on the bed and picked up each piece one by one. My head hurt, I felt fuzzy and off, and yet it felt familiar. I remembered this feeling.

As I rushed to get dressed, I was trying to recall the evening to understand how I ended up here, naked in bed with a married man. None of it made sense to me. As my mind went through all this, I rushed out his front door and noticed I was late for school. I was never late. I never missed. I took such pride in my education and efforts to submit my package.

I began walking down the street while calling for a ride. I felt such shame. *I am a homewrecker. What did I do?* I asked myself. I felt guilty. I felt naive. I felt embarrassed. The thoughts crowded my mind, pouring in faster than I could process them. Rapid breathing, trying to hold back tears, the thoughts took over and wouldn't stop. *I should have known something like this was going to happen! That poor boy! Why was I naked? Why do I feel this way? What happened? His wife is deployed, oh no, what did I do?*

I am a horrible person.

I showered as soon as I got home, trying to scrub away any reminder of him. I spent the day ashamed and trying to piece together the evening and how it led to the morning. It didn't make sense. It didn't add up. The noise in my head didn't stop for days. I didn't speak to anyone. I stayed quiet. I stayed quiet because it was my fault. I stayed quiet because that's what happens when people drink. I stayed quiet because I should have assumed his intentions when he offered to drive me home. I stayed quiet because I was ashamed I allowed this to happen. And I stayed quiet because I had a leadership team full of men who I felt I couldn't trust.

This changed me. This changed everything about me and how I would view the world, people, friends, men, and myself. This walked me right into my promiscuous era. The era where I didn't care anymore. No self-respect, no self-worth, no value for self. I was a damn good mom, though; Nattie would never see it. She would never know the pain I was feeling. I tucked it all away while she was around. I have my childhood to thank for being able to compartmentalize so well. I became the girl who jumped from relationship to relationship, partner to partner, searching for someone to make me feel safe in my own body. Searching for someone to see the value in me, because I certainly didn't. I became the sidepiece, the girl who felt loved when a *man* chose her over his current partner. I welcomed this because it was better than being alone. It was all I felt I deserved.

Another holiday weekend and I happened to swing by Steven's to check on him; I had heard through other friends that he was having a hard day. I was so worried about all my friends, especially those post-combat. I knocked on the door and he answered and let me in. As we walked from the entryway to the living room, I could tell he was under the influence. He looked disheveled, had an unsteady gait, and was talking gibberish.

When I asked if he was okay, he snapped. The look in his eyes was scary. He was there and he wasn't, all in the same breath. As I asked what was wrong, he started moving toward me. I began to get nervous and could feel my heart picking up speed, but tried to remind myself I had nothing to worry about. He continued toward me and I backed up and found myself up against the dining room wall. Scanning the room for a potential exit, next thing I knew he had his hands around my neck choking me, speaking in another language. I was gasping for air and trying to fight back but he was strong. I kneed him one last time, and he finally released his tight grip from my neck.

Gasping for air and shoving him away from me, I ran out the front door. I felt him chasing me. I was running and screaming for help. All of a sudden a fellow coworker, Jeremiah, heard me, saw me running, and immediately darted in my direction. I ran down three flights of stairs, losing my flip flops in the process. As I ran through bushes, stepping on what felt like every single thorn, Jeremiah was able to pin Steven down, stopping him in his tracks. I pounded on another friend's door in the complex and they answered. I was crying hysterically, feet torn up, and scared shitless. My friend and Jeremiah escorted Steven back to his apartment and kept a watch over him as he passed out and slept off whatever he had consumed. I was escorted to the after-hours clinic, where a wound debridement was performed due to all the punctures in my feet from the bushes.

The next day I called Antwon and Jeremiah to check in on Steven, and he was still out of it. They said he was still sleeping pretty hard. The following week I went to work. I kept to myself. I was feeling a theme developing at the command—a constant state of shame, embarrassment, and naivety. I received flowers at work from Steven; he was extremely apologetic and could not account for his actions. He remembered small bits and pieces but, much like my own previous experiences, could not put the puzzle together.

In the midst of all this, I divorced Mike. My ex-husband was not seeing Nattie, he was not paying child support, and everything in both my professional and personal life was erupting. My mental health was at an all-time low.

Deep breath, Candice, you got this. You are almost to the finish line.

I stayed the course, hoping and praying all would work out in my favor. And then the results came back. I was selected for MECP and would be checking out of that command an entire year early. I only had to make it through six more months. In that time, I distanced myself from the clinic "friends," connected with others I had met along my path, and continued to focus on Nattie and how I wanted life to look in this new season of our life.

This season in my life showed me just how much of a caregiver and protector I was, even when it was not warranted. I had such a strong desire to feel loved, valued, and accepted that I was willing to do or be anything to anyone, even if that meant devaluing myself. If I could go back and hug this version of myself, I don't know if I would ever let go. I have carried so much shame, grief, and pain as a result of these few events. There were so many opportunities for me to course correct, but I didn't realize the depth of my depression. The depth of my pain. And how with each decision to stay the course, I self-sabotaged and abandoned myself that much more. To the reader who sees themselves in this chapter, I see you and I witness you.

PERMISSION GRANTED to transform pain into power.

The Reckoning Era

"This isn't the time to let up or give up."

—Sarah Hunt-Blackwell

It was time for a fresh start. New beginnings were becoming a theme in my life.

I was proving everyone wrong:

Dad: You'll never be anything when you grow up.

Me: I was just accepted into an Officer program.

High School Counselor: You'll never get into a four-year college.

Me: I was just accepted into three four-year college nursing programs.

Me: I am not smart enough. I am not good enough.

Also Me: I fucking did the thing. I am doing the fucking thing!

It came down to me believing in me. It came down to me counting on me. I was finally granting myself permission to receive success and happiness. I was so proud of achieving this goal. It was the start of something beautiful blossoming. As the summer months passed, I continued working on myself to prepare for the challenge of MECP. I saved money, I connected with the college, I went to church, I prayed, I was deeply devoted to my daughter, and I stayed focused on the vision of becoming an officer.

During the first semester of school, as I attempted to get acclimated and find my rhythm, I struggled with my studies. I had always memorized what I needed to know back in high school to make it through. That approach was not working, and I found myself second guessing on my quizzes and tests. I spent so much time studying, my friends even spent weekends helping me. It was like a door was closed off to the part of my brain that I needed to access to understand the material. I would take Nattie to Kangaroo Jac's on the weekends so she could burn off energy jumping around and playing for hours, while I sat there and made notecard after notecard. I felt less guilt because I knew she was having fun.

Suddenly it was winter break; I'd made it through one of many semesters. Just as soon as I started celebrating, I received news my grandmother had passed. I loved her so much. It was like she could always see the pain and injustice when she looked into my eyes. I believe she had an intuitive gift that I don't think she openly shared with others.

Nattie and I headed to Chicago where we all celebrated her life. While there, I had an experience I will never forget. I went to bed, drifting off into my dreams. Asleep, I felt a presence and woke up. And then in this strange but beautiful moment, I saw a girl. Very angelic. She had blonde hair, with ringlet curls. She was floating and very young. She had the most beautiful smile. I felt so peaceful and carried. She was surrounded in a glow of pure white. I felt hypnotized and full of love. Then suddenly I heard, "It's not your fault."

From there, I was watching a scene play out. I saw myself in what appeared to be a kitchen and a young toddler was in a highchair. She was yelling and screaming, throwing food at my face. I watched that version of me tend to the toddler. My face looked so heavy, dull, sad, and frustrated. I immediately had a sensation rush over me that she was sick. *My unborn daughter, my Haley Elizabeth, was sick. I could not have lived out my purpose had she been born.* She was there to teach me what deep love and sacrifice was. She made me appreciate so much in that small time we shared together.

I remember waking up and feeling so many emotions. I was sad because I wanted more time with her. I was confused at what had just happened, how I was *awake* and looking at her while somehow also watching what felt like a scene from a movie playing out right in front of me. I felt honored that she loved both me and my purpose here on Earth enough to sacrifice herself for the greater good. *I felt proud.* Proud I'd created something so beautiful and selfless. I felt joy because I knew this was my grandmother's doing. Her transition and reunion with Haley allowed for this beautiful closure to take place, releasing the guilt I had been carrying.

I woke up the next morning still in shock. We got to the wake and as we stood in line, someone was passing out what appeared to be a bookmark. It was beautiful. I flipped it over and about fell to my knees. There was an angel, and she looked identical to the one I had seen the night before. There she was, my Haley Elizabeth, stamped on this bookmark. A bookmark I knew I would never get rid of. I wanted her energy, her face, always a small reach away.

Into the new year and new semester, I was really gaining some momentum in this student life. I had a flow, I was developing balance, and I had time for Nattie and time for myself to unwind and refill my cup. My grades were steady and I was really feeling proud of the place I was at in my life. I kind of felt like I could finally take a deep breath. *Inhale, exhale, you got this, Candice.*

This season allowed time with friends. Laughing, BBQs, dancing—those things that really lit me up. I even started dating someone again. Goodness, was he a catch... he loved the outdoors, played baseball, had a great personality, was funny and handsome, and seemed too good to be true. We went very slowly. I was so focused on Nattie, school, and getting good grades that I was determined to not let anyone or anything disrupt that. We connected and really enjoyed our time together.

Time crept by. He went away for a week but shortly after he returned, he was different. I knew this *different,* as I had experienced it with multiple boyfriends over the past few years. We had a discussion, and he broke up with me. It was over just like that. I remember being so heartbroken. Such a lost girl, moving through the hustle culture trying to provide for her daughter. Someone just wanting to be seen, be heard, be loved. It felt like that was never going to come to fruition. So far out of reach and not meant for me.

I started watering the seeds again. *Why was I not enough? Why was I unlovable? What did I do wrong?*

I came home from school one day to notice something on my door. I had been served. I was being sent to court due to Mike not paying his bills, which I was still technically a co-signer on. Because he was no longer in the military and was living out of state, they could not track him down. *Oh, the peaks and valleys of life.*

I was already secured with a lawyer due to the child support issues, so she took this case on as well. We went to court and it was disclosed to me that the notes for the motorcycle and truck he had purchased had not been paid for months. The court made the decision to garnish my wages, just under a thousand dollars per month to cover his payments and a percentage of the rearages. A million thoughts flooded my head all at the same time. *How am I going to pay this? How will I be able to pay all the other bills? This is not fair!* I wasn't even getting paid two thousand dollars every paycheck, and now over half my pay was going toward my mortgage and *his* bills. The garnishment was more than my mortgage payment.

A single mother trying to make ends meet, while also paying for my ex's bills, I found myself having to work a second job on my days off. The place that offered this much flexibility was a bar and restaurant about two miles from my house. I applied and got the job starting the next day. It was such a weird experience because I had not worked in an environment like this before; it was polar opposite to what I was used to. I slowly allowed my personality to creep out. I got into a flow getting to know the regulars, the menu, and the drink selection. I inched my way into blending in with the other girls, going from mid-thigh shorts to little mini-skirts with spandex tights.

I made good money, and slowly but surely I found my way around and became one of the top sales generators for that location. I had regulars that came just to see me, all healthy customer relationships who tipped well. I brought conversation, intellect, and a fun and playful personality, but left behind the hustle-and-grind mentality. I loved working there. Little did I know how much joy it would bring me to get outside of the military network and actually vibe with people I usually wouldn't. I found it empowering, giving myself permission to let this side of me surface.

It was a Friday night. I had just finished my shift when I received a photo of my close friend Sarah out with my most recent ex. Since it was the summer, Nattie was away with her dad, so I decided to stay after work and hang out on the patio where a live band was playing. My boss, Miles, came up to me because he saw I looked upset. I shared what had happened and he was kind and bought me a drink. My friend showed up to meet me there, and we chatted over what felt like betrayal while sipping redheaded sluts (my cocktail of choice at the time). Next came the crying. Yep, I was that girl, at the bar half schnockered, sobbing over the assumed betrayal of a best friend and an ex.

Another blow to my self-esteem and self-worth. Feeling not good enough turned into a night at Miles' home with a bunch of my other coworkers. I woke up the next morning doing the walk of shame, again. *Why do I not learn? Why is it that I try to replace one painful event with another? You know better, Candice!* I remembered every detail of the night before, but the dopamine hit of feeling wanted, even if it was just to be used in that moment, soothed me. That night was the start of an extremely dark period in my life.

The convenience of Miles living right behind me had us moving more quickly than normal. I struggled with this relationship because his position often had him connected to women; it was his position as manager that other vulnerable girls like me felt pulled to. He constantly reassured me that I had nothing to worry about, that he wasn't interested in anyone else. But my intuition spoke differently. He told me repeatedly I was overreacting. There were many nights I would question his behavior out of insecurity, or because of something I saw or overheard. I would be gaslit and hushed. I found myself up against the sliding glass door many nights with his hand on my chest and clavicle area, telling me, "I would never hurt you, why are you doing this, Candice, I love you. Why are you acting this way? Why don't you believe me? Why are you doing this? I don't want to fight with you."

I believe in all my heart, even to this day, he had deep love for me. Or that's what I told myself because to me, love meant chaos, confusion, and fighting. That was what was familiar. His behavior was retraumatizing, often leading me back to my past assaults and my childhood.

As time passed, I started to feel under a microscope, controlled. One morning I went into the living room to say goodbye for the day. He met me with, "Who are you getting all dressed up for?" because I was in something other than a hoodie and jeans. I remember him giving me so much grief for it; I felt guilty, thinking maybe I was giving off the wrong impression. After my first class, I drove all the way home, changed into a hoodie, jeans, and flip flops, and put my hair up in a bun to make him feel better. I was constantly accused of cheating on him with guy friends I had... to the point I stopped hanging out with them because the arguments just weren't worth it to me. Isolated. Alone. Controlled. Denying my reality. I was in a deep depression.

Then it happened. I received an email from a girl I worked with, Carrie, disclosing how she had slept with him. She wanted to let me know because she felt bad about it. I remember being so distraught. I don't think it was necessarily the thought of losing him that distressed me, but more the fact that it was happening again. I was being cheated on yet again. The rejection. This was all I knew about relationships—they all cheated on me. Relationships, better yet men, were *not safe. Men all leave. They all think I am not good enough, skinny enough, or pretty enough.*

I was done. I was so tired of being treated like this. Believing the words of men who didn't value or appreciate me and everything I had to offer. I remember that night going out to a pizza joint with my friend. I just danced my heart out. It was what I did. And of course, not long after being there, Miles showed up. My other ex-boyfriend was also there, so I just danced and drank to ease my pain. To numb myself from it all. I was tired of feeling this pain. Each time it happened, the *not good enough* root got longer, wider, and deeper. The roots were spreading.

My ex-boyfriend and I ended up back at my place together and, of course, reconnected for another hit of dopamine, another attempt to validate my worth and to make myself feel good in that now moment. The next morning when I woke up, I suddenly realized I deserved more. I continued to ignore his calls and messages, determined to refocus.

The weekend was here. I wasn't feeling well and as the day went on, it worsened. I was so lethargic and nauseous, and I had a headache. My muscles and joints ached; something didn't feel right. I kept telling myself I was coming down with a cold and that I would just take it easy, rest up, and feel better in the morning. Nattie was my distraction! We went to a friend's house and she reconnected with her little sassy clan of friends, watching *Dora The Explorer* while I observed the changes in my body.

The next morning I had a friend take me to the clinic. By this point I was extremely sick, could barely walk, and was on fire everywhere. I feared what was happening but had a guess. The doctor swabbed me and gave me instructions moving forward. I was so sick; I wish my experience on no one. I laid on the couch in my own misery, realizing this was my fault. In my own effort to self-soothe, to feel valued and wanted, I'd managed to sabotage my own health and wellness. I crawled up and down my stairs. I fought a fever, back pain, leg pain, headaches, and horrible, gosh-awful pain in my female region. Nattie was so well-behaved. I don't think she thought anything other than, "*Momma is sick with a cold.*"

I got a call that week and was told I had a sexually transmitted disease—herpes simplex, to be exact. Something I would now carry for the rest of my life because of one reckless moment. Absolutely devastated, I thought, *I deserve this; that's what I get for having sex with my ex.* I beat myself up and punished myself for days, and even missed an entire week of school because I could barely stand or walk without getting winded, lightheaded, and dizzy. I was a mess. I was a wreck, depressed, and in a place I never would have imagined myself ever being.

Journal Entry

I believe our felt sense of worth is a direct reflection of the relationships we have with others. I was so concerned with having someone and feeling wanted and loved, I didn't care how that looked. Someone, anyone, save me.

I cared more about others and their feelings than myself. Decaying and crumbling piece by piece, I gave away myself, my authority, and my heart and love everytime I dismissed their abusive actions as they demonstrated their own version of love.

I carried such shame and guilt for years, having not done *the work,* which led to irresponsible and self-destructive behaviors. I share these stories with you hoping I will catch your attention before you go off and make similar (if not the same) reckless, self-destructive choices. And if you have *been there, done that* and can relate, I witness and share this with you: you are not your mistakes. You don't need the love, affection, or attention of a man to be whole. You are whole all on your own. While I am not thrilled to live with this disease the rest of my life, and it makes for awkward conversations, it has been a saving grace. It has allowed me to develop self-discipline, to learn other ways to cope through relationship challenges, and to practice discernment in who I wish to share my time and space with. Remember, Reader, this is just another season. Weed out what is not needed; plant, water, and nourish new seeds; and watch them grow.

PERMISSION GRANTED to heal and honor your true value.

The Breaking Free Era

"Seeing unhealthy patterns in your family and deciding that those patterns end with you and will not be passed down to future generations, is an extremely brave & powerful decision.

—Tiny Tot

Time passed, and Miles asked to get back together. He said things would be different this time. That he would stop going out and stay in. That he just wanted a family. That he missed me and that I was worth it. I contemplated long and hard about it, and ended up deciding that unless I wanted to be alone forever, I had better accept. I was contaminated… I was gross. No one would want a divorced single mom with a lifelong STD, so I took him back. I *forgave* him for his treatment of me, for his cheating, for his awful cutthroat words I heard on the regular. It took some time for me to let my guard down. I didn't trust him; I was always looking over my shoulder at work, wondering what conversations he was having with females. It just never stopped. On top of that, he still accused me of doing what he had done to me. Now I get why he always tried to control me—it was because he was not being faithful, projecting his own insecurities onto me. This was not a healthy relationship, but a codependency with a rescue-like bond; in sum, a trauma-bond.

Another day, another argument, so Miles decided he would go to his house after work. I got home at 2:30 a.m., so I shut and locked my screen door. *Weird*, I thought, as I had never locked that screen before. I changed into my comfy, oversized hoodie and sweatpants and curled up on the couch with my pharmacology book to study for the quiz that was scheduled in just eight hours. I heard a knock on my door, which confused me because of the time. I opened the door to find a ginormous man in all black. He was *huge.*

"Hi there," he said. "My car is broken down on the side of the highway, up the road, and I wondered if you could write me a check so I can pay for a tow truck."

Trying to remain calm, I was scared while also navigating the situation. "Sir, I am going to call my boyfriend so he can help." I called Miles. He thought I was making the entire story up as a way to get him over to my house. Heart racing, shallow breaths, sweaty palms, and some quick thinking, I said, "Sir, my boyfriend doesn't have a check but can come over with cash."

The man rattled at my front screen as if he was trying to open it and enter my home.

"I am grabbing my roommate and will be right over," Miles said.

"Sir, my boyfriend is on his way over with a friend to help you."

Suddenly, the man said he would wait in his car. He began walking toward the dead end cul de sac of my street.

Less than a minute had gone by and Miles and his roommate came running from the gap between my house and my neighbor's. I pointed to the direction of where the man went, and a car was driving from the cul de sac with its headlights turned off, headed in our direction. The man was in his car driving to escape the wrath of these two three-hundred-pound men that had come to help me. This man's car was not broken down on the highway up the road. This man's car was running just fine. This man was not at my home for money. *This man was at my home for me.*

This experience watered the seeds of *I am not safe.* This man robbed me of any safety I felt in my own home. He planted seeds of fear. I spent days and days looking over my shoulder. *What if my daughter had been home? How would I protect her? Is she safe? Should I sell my home and move?*

I sometimes find myself reflecting back to that day, and I end up in a rabbit hole of what-ifs. I find myself so grateful that I had people so close by who were willing to put themselves at risk to help me. I am forever grateful for Miles coming that night. In these reflective moments, it also reminds me just how massive my purpose is here on Earth. I have almost met death a few times, and to be saved each time is to know the power of my purpose.

Fast forward to January: a new semester was beginning, and I was happy to put that year to rest. It was a brutal one with many lessons learned. I rang in the new year with the anticipation of getting my associates degree come the end of spring, which was a huge milestone for me. It represented *almost there*, one degree down and one to go.

But because we live life in peaks and valleys, what goes up must come down. Still getting monthly outbreaks due to my STD, I started feeling off toward the end of January, beginning of February. I assumed it was another outbreak in progress. I was still fairly new to these experiences, and they kind of seemed and felt different each time. But this time, as a couple days passed, I noticed some other things that just didn't add up. Sure enough, I was pregnant. I went upstairs to find Miles sleeping. I woke him to share the news and his face absolutely lit up. He was so thrilled and excited. Me, not so much. I just couldn't shake our history thus far and my fear of what was to come. Once the initial shock wore off, I knew from past experiences to enjoy it all. My miscarriage having occurred four years prior, I knew to be grateful, no matter the uncertainty and fear that riddled my body's core. I knew this child had a purpose and I was going to see it through, and I knew I was going to love him regardless of where Miles and I stood.

I no longer worked at the bar and restaurant, so I spent lots of time alone since he was still working. When he wasn't working, he was paying off his sentence for a DUI he had received. He served time part of the week and then worked his shifts the rest of the week. It felt pretty lonely and, man, that felt familiar.

We slowly moved into a constant back and forth within the relationship. I didn't care for the bar scene, I didn't like how much he worked, and I didn't see this being something that was healthy and going to last. And, of course, everything was always my fault, anyways—the insecure, mouthy, emotional, hormonal pregnant girl.

During this time, Miles was also committed to stopping some of his habits in order to better support his health. I remember going out with my friend Randi for dinner one evening, and we decided to swing by and surprise Miles at work. Outside next to the security and bouncers, there he was, smoking. This was something he claimed he'd stopped. When I confronted him when he got home, he lied right to my face. It made no sense because he knew I saw him. I was so upset. I felt like, if he was going to lie about that, what else was he lying about? *Maybe I was overreacting,* I told myself.

I went to bed alone upstairs as he fell asleep, like most nights, downstairs on my living room chair. I remember crying myself to sleep, questioning if I was purposely nitpicking because I was not happy. I constantly questioned my reality. Self-doubt ran rampant. It felt as though I was constantly told what I saw or heard was not actually what I saw and heard. It truly felt like a total mind fuck many days.

I woke up and it was Sunday morning. I snatched Nattie and we headed off to church. I remember telling my friend Lori that I needed change. After I explained what had happened, she offered empathy and was just present. Her energy of just being there meant everything that day. We left from church service and pulled aside the pastor's wife. We talked privately about my situation and how I felt so alone and lost. She reminded me that I was a child of God, that he had his hands on me, and that it would all work out. She reminded me that I was strong just for being able to come to service that day. From there, Lori went home and I made arrangements with another ex of Miles, who agreed to watch Nattie while I handled my personal business.

I dropped Nattie off while I did what had to be done. I could not take the chance of my children experiencing or witnessing what I had growing up. I walked into my home, dead set on ending our relationship. I was choosing my children. I was scared. I was nervous. My body was on guard. But one step in front of the other, remembering the pastor's wife's words that God's hand was on me, I walked through the door.

I initiated the conversation by asking if we could talk about the night before. Very assertively he said something to the tune of, "I didn't do anything wrong," and further explained why he'd had the cigarette. I remember sharing with him that it went beyond the cigarette: that I didn't trust him and felt like I was just overall unhappy. He did not receive that well. Raising his voice at me, he started calling me names: fat, cunt, bitch. As I stood there unaffected, I think it upset him more. I continued my stance that we were over and that he needed to leave. That is when he spit at me standing a little bit across the room from him. I had a nasty comment back to him while also reminding myself I was carrying a sweet child and I didn't need to get all stressed out. Breathing and saying my prayers to myself, I let him know once again where I stood. He pushed me. I knew I needed to call Lori. We already had a plan mapped out that if I called, she would be on her way.

He went upstairs, and I remember moving to the landing of my stairs. I wanted to keep an eye on what was happening. I didn't know if he was packing his belongings or what. As he came down, we got into another verbal argument as he continued to call me names. He then placed his hand on my face and pushed with force, jerking my face to the side. It left a handprint on my left cheek.

Shortly thereafter, Lori arrived. Miles told Lori she needed to leave. She told him she would not be going anywhere without me and remained in the doorway. As he went upstairs he leaned over the side banister and spit on me. It landed on my eye and dripped down my face as I stood there, almost sick. Lori yelled at him, but he told her to mind her own business. I was yelling at him, because I was still in shock he was behaving this way, while at the same time not surprised at all. I immediately thought, *This is what I feared life would be like with him permanently.* I had lived it already as a child.

I asked him to leave, but he refused. This was MY house. I owned it. We were not renting it. He was not a cosigner or on a joint lease. But he refused to leave. I just needed to get out before things escalated, so I left with Lori. I found comfort in sitting with her. She helped me remember my truth. She helped me to account for what had happened, because I was questioning at that point if he had even touched me, or if he had spit on me. She had to repeatedly tell me what she saw to help convince me of what I knew all along: that she saw him spit from the top of the stairs. That she heard him call me a fat cunt bitch. That she saw the red marks on my face.

I made a phone call to Billy, a friend I had stopped talking to while with Miles, hoping we could crash there for a night or two. Billy had been alongside me for years through it all. He could be trusted, and I felt safe with him. He allowed Nattie and I to stay with him so we could have a safe haven. A couple days turned into a couple weeks. I had popped over to my house a few times throughout those couple weeks, and it was clear Miles was still staying there. Garbage scattered, clothes everywhere, beer bottles… it was frustrating he just assumed I would return and he could stay there, while I was displaced and inconveniencing someone else. I gave myself permission to take back my power. I drove to my home to see his car was not there, so I went in. I quickly went through my house and placed all the items of his I could find into garbage bags. I tied them up and placed them into my car, drove a couple miles to his place of employment in broad daylight, and placed his belongings on top of his car.

I really felt bad for doing it that way, but I felt as if he left me no choice. It was clear I was done, as I had told him. I also told him I wanted him to leave, which he refused. I didn't want to call the cops, because with his record I knew he would get into trouble. I knew this was all deeply rooted pain, and I just triggered things in him he didn't want to accept. I know the rescuer and fixer in me runs deep. This was the only way I knew to remove him from my home and do it in a civil way. But I had to choose myself. Really, it was Nattie and my unborn child I was choosing.

The coming days were spent focusing on school, Nattie, and attending doctors' appointments. I remember the first one I went to was by myself. I was so depressed, I cried; I shared with the nurse how alone I felt. She was a godsend. She comforted me and offered me support services and other resources that paved the way for the other side of what I was experiencing.

During this time, I also dealt with the ramifications of being an ex of Miles. The fabricated stories, lies, photos of naked women he was lying next to, while in the next breath receiving drunk texts saying how much we can make it work and that he loved and missed me. There were many nights he came knocking on my door drunk at 5 a.m., yelling for me to let him in. It was exhausting. I felt like I was going to break while also having discipline and my vision set on graduating. I could see it: me walking across the stage and getting my degree. I just had to keep seeing it. I had to keep saying it out loud. I had to keep going to church. I had to keep rooting for me. I had to keep giving myself permission to move forward.

Now in my bachelor year, I knew I was due anytime, so I worked as much as I could between school work and housework so that I would have a natural flow into the transition. I was scared to death—I'd found out the new baby was a boy, and I didn't know boys like I knew girls. When I was dilated and contractions were increasing, my dad offered to fly into town. He didn't like the fact I was by myself, and he knew my situation with Miles. While I was at school he organized my cupboards and pantry, and cleaned the entire house. I was mowing the lawn until thirty-seven weeks pregnant, so he decided he would take over that job and did one more final sweep of the yard. We walked around the pond and even went to the mall to walk and hopefully get things moving. It felt really good, and I felt supported having him with me. He didn't drink, which was also a huge surprise; it had been a daily thing for him for as long as I could remember.

Sharing this, it makes me sad that I harbored so much anger toward him, and that I didn't give myself permission to notice or recognize his love for me. It was like I was determined to keep the narrative in my head that I was less than, not enough, which prevented me from truly seeing the times he did try to be there for me.

While in class, I went into labor. I called my dad to let him know, and I also called Miles so he knew and could be ready. When I got home from school, I showered, grabbed my bag and carseat, and was ready to go. It was a long, painful labor and delivery due to his positioning. The nurse worked with me for hours turning side to side to get him to move. After what felt like the entire duration of the pregnancy, he finally corrected positioning and I had some relief. Because of that, I progressed pretty quickly, and before I knew it I had my amazing Zander Anthony. My heart melted.

Sitting on the bed in the hospital room I felt incredible sadness. Feeling alone, I cried while telling myself how I was proving my father right: I was turning out like my mom. Failed relationship after failed relationship, two different fathers to my kids, STD, abusive relationships—I was becoming her. Tears fell. All I could do was look at Zander, knowing I had to do better. Whatever I needed to do, it had to happen. Both kids deserved it.

I went to the hospital and gave birth on a Thursday, was discharged Saturday, and back to school full time by Monday. The entire experience brought me a new level of awareness and insight into what the future was going to look like. I had this deep knowing that moving forward, it was me and both my kids. Just the three of us. I felt acceptance, but also worried how I was going to financially afford everything. I remember crying in that hospital room all by myself while Zander slept into his deep-sleep, post-colostrum coma. It angered me that Mike was buying new cars and taking trips, and I was paying his bills and raising his daughter with what felt like zero support. I was angry that Miles was able to still have the freedom to do all the things and spend his money freely on his new girlfriend, while I didn't get any financial support preparing for Zander. It made me look at why my mom raised us to be so independent. She always said to set yourself up so you never have to rely on a man. I was starting to understand her message, because I surely couldn't count on either of them. At least now I knew what I needed to do in order to ensure my two kids were taken care of. I moved forward and hired an attorney to sue Mike, since we had legal paperwork declaring his responsibility to those bills. This was a start to not giving a flying fuck about neither Miles' nor Mike's feelings, and moving into mommy-mode and protector-mode. I had spent so much of my life protecting others — it was time to protect my own.

Zander: I loved him so much, but man, oh, man, I struggled doing this alone. The days and nights were long and sleepless. I finally figured out a flow that worked for us — and by us I mean the many friends that stepped in to help me watch my kids while I finished up that fall semester, as well as the one in the spring. Those months were filled with chaos, stress, doubt, and fear. We were in some challenging semesters that were didactically heavy, requiring my friends to spend time after school hours breaking it all down in a way my brain could understand. I was sleep deprived. I was working out a lot in order to pass the physical fitness test in preparation for officer development school, dealing with two court issues for child support, and trying to make ends meet.

That winter I remember sitting in my car, because my electricity got turned off due to non-payment, discovering the dollar menu was in fact the most cost effective, and bringing *running on fumes* a whole new meaning — that car drove at times it should have been immobile. Seeing this happen in real time, with no recourse or ability to control it, brought me so much shame. But it also brought anger, because if I was not having to support these kids alone, it would have made such a difference in the way we lived. I kept the end goal in sight. I kept focusing on the vision. I had just a short time left until we were to reap the benefits of hard work and sacrifices. We had this! I gave myself permission to stay focused no matter how many times I wanted to throw in the towel.

As the semester was closing out, after a long process, many court hearings, and lots of money for a lawyer, I was informed I won the case against Mike and he had to pay $20,000 over the course of time and $25,000 (which was actually the cost he owed) if he did not meet the judge's deadline date. On top of paying that, he was also obligated to pay child support, which was a separate case we were navigating.

This chapter I broke free from the generational pattern of domestic violence. This had been woven through my lineage for years based on stories from grandparents, what I witnessed during my childhood, and my own account of enduring abuse. I chose to have better. I chose for my children to have better. I discovered how powerful I am, even in the midst of darkness where I can't seem to see the light. I learned to receive and welcome love, help, and support from the angels God placed in front of me on earth, a pure extension of him and his love. Reader, if you see yourself here, regardless of the piece that resonates, know you, too, can do this. You are powerful beyond measure. You are stronger than you will ever know.

PERMISSION GRANTED to transform and thrive.

The Foundation Era

"Some of life's best moments are the unexpected ones."

—Susan Gale

I couldn't believe I did it; I was off to officer training. As excited as I was to start this next season in my life, I was met with worry and sadness leaving both of my children. We all know what happened the last time I had to leave for military training. I remained open-minded to the experience, as I knew it would be different from the enlisted bootcamp I had attended nine years prior.

Arriving, I remember how big the main area was. The large building that smelled like your grandma's attic chest of drawers. The stairs—ugh, the stairs! We took the stairs for everything, and there were so many floors—of course with my roommates and I living on the top. We found ourselves congregating in the evenings in the laundry room. We would sit around a table talking and polishing our boots, making jokes about who messed up, or playfully pointing out what someone did wrong and how many pushups we all had to do because of it. We were pretty friendly with one another. We all got along, joked, and even hung out together in our free time on the weekends.

One day in class, we broke into groups based on the corps we were a part of. As a nurse, we met with a senior leader who gave us an idea of what we could expect as we checked into our new duty stations. During our informational session, we discovered who in our corps would be going to the same duty stations. This is when I officially met Keith. Also getting stationed where I was, we started to chitchat in the laundry room, which eventually led to chichat on our liberty. We became friends pretty quickly. *Those were the days, the beginning of something beautiful.*

Once graduating, we made our way to our next assignment. I made it back just in time to make Natalya's dance recital! I had missed her and Zander so much. Now a newly commissioned officer, O1, and checking into the very command I checked into as a newly enlisted sailor, E1, I was beginning a new journey. I was excited, proud, and nervous. *I can't believe I really did it,* I told myself. Flooded with emotions and the words of those who thought I couldn't do it, I really had to let it soak in. I was in awe of myself and all I had navigated.

Settling in and getting back on a routine, I introduced Keith to all my friends so he had connection and community. I constantly played matchmaker for him and his new crush of the month that never worked out. Even though early on we had decided to keep our relationship friends only, part of me felt like I was starting to connect with him on a different level. *It was like I could see him.* And because there was no intention of becoming more, I could really see him.

It was Labor Day weekend, and we took a small road trip to celebrate. We all loaded up in the car, Keith included, and headed home to Sandusky, Ohio, to see my family. The smell of BBQ filled the house and backyard, the firepit provided us light and warmth, people chucked bags playing cornhole, and the rock music took me back to my childhood. *Those were the days.* Keith and I found ourselves walking down the sidewalk talking about us, our blooming relationship, and how we were so glad to have met one another. He stopped me in the middle of the sidewalk, and that is when he asked me—"Maybe we should give it a try. Let's make it official." I was so excited. He was genuine, smart, big hearted, direct, and honest.

This relationship was like something I had never experienced before. It was close to my birthday, and Keith wanted to treat me. It was a fall day with crisp air, and we loaded into his Mazda Sport and rode down to a nearby ski shop. My body got excited; I loved skiing. He took me inside, and told me to pick out my ski gear. I remember walking around the store, not knowing what to look at or what to grab; I felt uncomfortable. *This was unfamiliar.* His level of generosity was not something I had experienced before or felt I deserved. I felt apprehensive to pick up anything. He could see me struggling and walked over to help me decide on what to grab. He picked up goggles, hats, pants, even a jacket. His actions in that moment felt genuine. He was so safe.

I look back and see how quickly we moved as boyfriend and girlfriend since our foundation of friendship had been so strong. Keith always seemed to want to surprise me, which was an added layer in this romantic partnership. It was date night! Keith surprised me with a date to make us officially official; never being treated like this before, I was nervous. In my mind I kept asking, *What's the catch?* He took me to an amazing restaurant at the Oceanfront, where we had steak dinners, wine, and dessert, and took a romantic walk on the beach. We came back to the room to my favorite flowers and a card with him asking me to be his girlfriend with the cutest "check yes, no, or maybe" on it like in grade school.

The next morning we woke up and decided to take a walk on the beach. I vividly remember the warm sand between my toes as my feet sank into it with each step. The smell of the ocean water while hearing the waves crash upon the shore. The gentle kiss of the sun as it shined down on us from above. This felt good. *Wow,* I thought. That's it. That is when things started to feel charged for me. My thoughts *ran,* not walked, through my mind. Conversations my dad had with Keith, telling Keith I had too much going on in my world, too much baggage. *He is settling with me because all the other girls weren't interested in him, so being with me is better than being alone.* I invited all them in, all the thoughts that fueled my belief of not being good enough. The chaos was my safety. The chaos was my certainty. Something in my life I could always rely and count on.

Keith tried reassuring me; he tried to convince me that my dad's opinion didn't matter and that those were not his thoughts. Deep down I didn't believe it. My body felt hot, my stomach felt gutted; I was having such an internal conflict with myself all while walking on the beach. Wanting to just be present and feel that kiss of the sun again, I couldn't get them to shut off. I kept yelling at myself to *just put a pin in them. Candice, you are self-sabotaging again.* I continued to tell myself, *if I mess this up now then I don't have to worry about when he will hurt me and do me like all the others have.* The thoughts continued. *I am not as skinny, pretty, or as smart as the other girls he was interested in earlier. I have two kids with two different men. I have an STD and am contaminated.* The stories continued pouring out of me, reinforcing all the reasons why I was *not enough* and *too much* all in the same breath.

I shamed myself for days while also pretending I was okay. I kept hearing my dad's voice as if I was proving him right. The baggage, how I was so much to manage. I felt myself start to disconnect and pull away. I wanted too much to protect my heart and my kids from someone getting too close, only to realize it was too much for him.

Looking back with the knowledge I have now, I had zero business being in a relationship. It was built on friendship but rooted in fear. What I mean is that it was rooted in all my lived experiences thus far, setting the tone for what would be. While I was trying to reprogram that not all men were going to hurt me, leave me, cheat on me, I began feeling like maybe I could let my guard down. We were Keith and Candice. We were a team, a united front conquering all the shit that came our way. And let me tell you, there are days I remember where I still cannot believe we made it out alive. It was a constant state of survival. Survival to get through the day. Survival to get through the tough conversations with exes. Survival supporting my mom. I felt like, at every corner I turned, someone needed something from me. Either that, or I placed that pressure on myself because of my caregiver tendencies. I was conditioned at such a young age to serve others over serving myself.

This made it difficult in our relationship because I struggled to allow him to be of service to me. I wholeheartedly believe he shows his love through acts of service. It was hard to allow a man to take care of me. I was a hyper-independent alpha female, and the idea of succumbing to a man meant I was getting weak. It meant I had to surrender and trust, and I just wasn't fully there. Too many times I had been proven right in that all men leave, that they will hurt me, and are not safe. My childhood taught me never to rely on a man because you will always end up disappointed in the end. I knew I needed to shift. I knew that the narrative taught to me as a child was wrong and was certainly not serving me. I needed to learn softness and femininity, and to learn how to welcome and receive, just as I gave. I had never been taken care of like this before. I felt so lucky and so confused all at the same time.

Fast forward to the spring, and I learned I was pregnant. We had just talked about kids and decided we were not interested in having more. Little did we know, one was already in the making. We had such a great conversation about what this would look like. He already had my engagement ring picked out, and was just waiting on the custom carving to be finished before proposing. Everything was already in motion.

As we navigated twelve-hour shift work, rotating schedules, back and forth night shifts and day shifts every six weeks, working weekends and holidays, getting Nattie to her soccer or dance, maintaining the house, dealing with exes, and navigating the pregnancy–which left me so sick–*we were exhausted*. Talk about burning the candle at both ends. The first trimester was just awful. I found myself in the emergency room for weakness and dehydration, and a couple times in the infusion clinic receiving banana bags. Because of my laboratory results, had Keith and I not been nurses stationed there, they were going to admit me. It was a long pregnancy between morning sickness and then being placed on high-risk due to my child's overdeveloped kidneys. Labor was tolerable. All settled in, epidural, rest, and it was time. I progressed quickly, and after a few pushes, our amazingly strong Broc Andrew was here. Keith was unable to cut the cord because it was wrapped twice around Broc's neck, but we got a cry out of him and our family was officially complete.

In the days and months to come I felt so incredibly blessed. I had a man who woke up through all hours and helped me feed Broc, change him, and took an honorable and active role in fathering him. I had been through it twice before without support like this. I could feel the love and gratitude deep in my heart. Appreciation flowed through my entire internal cavity. And, it scared me… really scared me. I would sink into the excitement and happiness of what we created. Then, suddenly, when I realized I was happy and living out this dream I never thought I deserved, fear riddled my entire core. I feared that it was all an illusion, that I was being naive to think this could be true, and that I was getting weak and dependent on a man.

As I returned from maternity leave, I was assigned to a new command where, for the first time since becoming an officer, I would be working a regular and routine Monday through Friday schedule. It was the final stretch of wedding planning, and we were excited for the normal and routine schedule we were now getting to live. What was supposed to be such a beautiful and magical time in our life turned out to be me living fully armed in my self-sabotage, once again.

This man, the epitome of amazing, and me, the epitome of scared. This doesn't mix. As time moved on, we grew more and more in our routine. We were more and more tired, more and more stressed out. The battle rhythm we once had was out of sync. We were moving on fumes. We would spend the weekend catching up and talking about our work day, what was going on, and the unloading of frustrations we both had given the stress, work, and desire to take a deep breath. Occasionally he would think he shared something with me, but he would realize it wasn't me but rather a female coworker. This was extremely activating for me. It made my throat tense and tight, my skin hot and flush, my heart racing, and made my breaths shallow and rapid. And then my mind would start ... *Oh no, here it is. I knew something felt off; I felt him pulling back. Why is he sharing such stories and details with her and not me?* My system was flooded and overwhelmed. *This was it. Time to armor up,* I told myself.

Journal Entry

Your self-worth is a pure reflection of all that is buried, or healed.

Don't be fooled by the persona you show others. Convincing yourself or others you're fine should be the red flag.

Unsolved problems, unhealed traumas, and unidentified events will eventually surface and explode when you least expect it too.

Sit in stillness. In the quiet of it all. See what arises within you. Allow yourself to feel it. Identify it. Name it. Then let go of it.

I didn't mention my feelings to him. I was afraid I would scare him off since he had already felt so annoyed with this same sort of behavior in the beginning. He wasn't the easiest to talk to about this specifically, and he always seemed to immediately get defensive. Hindsight, I am sure he was annoyed the conversation was still happening. Deep down I wanted to believe he wasn't the same, but I just couldn't get my brain to change its thinking. The fear was too deeply rooted. I shamed myself over and over because I couldn't reprogram these beliefs. I cried myself to sleep feeling helpless, like I didn't know how to just change it, feeling foolish. In order to meet an immediate need of connection, understanding, and safety, I connected with a friend. Something so innocent. Something to try to understand myself, my thinking, and to course correct. Instead, I cracked Keith's and my foundation, changing the course of our forever.

Maybe you have been on one or both sides of this chapter. Body riddled in confusion, the past surfacing and trying to provide you guidance, frustrated at the change you desire but can't seem to achieve. The *knowing* that things can be safe but yet you can't see in the dark to grab your life preserver. Armoring up to protect yourself when in reality all you are doing is subconsciously self-sabotaging. Rooted in fear, resisting the surrender. I see you, I am you. All these lived experiences live inside your internal cavity, driving your thoughts, action, and behaviors. It is not that you can't change, course correct, become one with your desired future—it's that you must first excavate what lives inside, so the mind can follow.

PERMISSION GRANTED to build a solid foundation for your new beginning.

The Realignment Era

"Seeds are planted everywhere,
it's the ones we choose to water that matter."

—Candice West

Relocating, we were excited to be near family. This had been the first time since I'd joined the military that we would be so close. My dad and his family were about forty-five minutes away, while my mom and that side of my family were around six hours. We were so excited to be close to join BBQs, birthday parties, and holiday season celebrations.

We arrived safe and sound, and divided and conquered having our house unpacked within the week. Decor hung, beds made, electronics all set up. We were ready to embark on this new adventure the military was offering us. But first, I needed to come clean. I knew it would be hard for him to hear, and would rip his heart out, but it wasn't something I could keep within. Most importantly, he deserved to know. We had such a sacred connection built on honesty, openness, and friendship at first. Sharing this violation of trust with him left me full of shame. I felt awful, like a terrible person. I thought to myself, *Is this what it felt like for the others who had betrayed me in the past?* It also led me to being vulnerable and soft, which was something I was conditioned to believe was not good or safe in relationships.

He met me with love and a response of self-accountability that I had not expected. He shared how we were a team and that it takes two for relationships to work, as well as to fall apart. It felt like the most genuine response, and one I didn't expect to receive. *I didn't deserve his love,* I told myself. I knew moving forward I would forever feel a sense of indebtedness to him for witnessing my entire heart in that moment.

And so the seed was planted: *I don't deserve love.* It took me days and weeks to view myself in a different light. The shame never dissipated. And though he didn't deserve this violation, I felt deep down that I deserved his forgiveness. I shared this very sentiment with Keith, that I am truly glad for this experience. It opened a door for me that I had not walked through in this way. With my first spouse, there had been so much between the both of us that fractured our relationship, but this relationship with Keith and I was not the same. I needed this to happen in this way, as painful, selfish, and destructive as it was. It allowed me to see my past partners for who they were—hurt individuals seeking safety and looking for their needs to be met, living in an active state of survival. Now, disagree as you may, but what I gained from that experience was a deeper understanding of hurt people, hurt people. *I was hurt.* And in an effort to feel safe, *I was hurting people.* In fact, I was becoming like those very people who had hurt me. Those moments where I had been *done wrong* in a relationship always left me feeling *not enough.* Whether it had been that I was not pretty enough, not skinny enough, not secure enough, _____ (fill in the blanks here), I know now that none of it was ever about me, and all about them. Chaos is what has been safe my entire life. Chaos was familiar. And when the chaos was no longer present in the same ways, when it subsided—when he seemed to have changed, when he was sharing things with the female coworker that he hadn't shared with me, when he felt withdrawn—my body did what it does best: the nervous system turned on and became fully activated, sensing a lack of safety. It was like a radar going off in my body telling me something was not right or okay. So, I did what I did best in those days and created the chaos, even though it was outside my character, my beliefs, and all I stood for. Even though I had been on the other side of those very circumstances, I craved chaos for internal safety.

This experience has served as a permission slip to take aligned action. To dig deep and locate the deeply rooted subconscious beliefs stored in my body to bring a deeper awareness of self. To give myself permission to start to heal those parts of me and move toward not only the forgiveness of others, but most importantly, the forgiveness of self. To this day, it still pains me that Keith had to be a part of my story in this way, and I am also so grateful he loved me and our family enough to recognize what I was bringing to him.

We moved on and continued our check-in process at the command. We had no idea what we were in for. I was told I would be the first active duty nurse to work at this location. The senior leader seemed hesitant to place me there, but as a prior-enlisted corpsman and a strong officer record, she felt determined I was the right one to step into the role. I walked to my unit, Keith at my side, and as I introduced myself I was met with abrasiveness from my new boss. Right off the bat I realized why the senior leader was hesitant in sending me to that unit. This boss of mine was a super assertive, hovering, aggressive human being.

I struggled so much at this command. I was met with constant questioning, didn't feel supported, lacked mentorship in the beginning, and felt all alone in this new role. But I also thrived on the challenge and the fact I was chosen. Me being chosen and being the first made me feel as if I was important. It felt like I mattered. For someone who felt the complete opposite her entire life, this lit me up. It made me want to do that much more and be that much better. But what I failed to realize is that the very woman who challenged me also made me angry and upset, and made me feel like I had no value or worth to the team. She was simply mirroring back to me how I truly felt about myself. But I was not in a place to know or even recognize it. I just saw a toxic passive aggressive woman. Little did I know I was her, and she was me.

Time moved on and suddenly there was a request for additional support to a remote location. Ten days later, I was boarding a plane and heading to another country to care for high-profile patients. I went from watching *Blues Clues* with my kiddos to living in another country for the next six months.

My team and I were not welcomed, liked, or supported by our patients. We worked twelve-hour shifts, and because of the manning we didn't have a set rotation like we could expect to have back in the States working at a medical center. We flipped back and forth from day shift to night shift, and every other weekend off was not guaranteed.

The days, weeks, and months were lonely. I had a small select group of friends, but nothing more. I wasn't really people's cup of tea. I was so fearful of making mistakes and getting into trouble that I followed the rules to a tee, whereas others in this high stress environment coped with the challenges by drinking, being promiscuous, and by taking risks in their relationships. I understood; I had been there a time or two in my life, too. This time I was determined to break the pattern. To do that, I continued my advanced education in the program I was enrolled in. I took a good handful of classes to keep focused on my long term goal and stayed busy, hoping it would make time pass quicker. Deployment was a mental and emotional mindfuck. I was not ready for that experience, but I was also ready at the same time thanks to my childhood.

Upon my return home there was clearly an adjustment period, but I feel like I fell seamlessly into the flow Keith had set in place over the six months I was away. I returned to working on the same unit with the same civilian boss and merged back into my role. At this point, I was about half-way complete with the tour and needed to focus on my next steps. I found it so challenging to be in the present, because I was always focused on the next evaluation, the next physical readiness test, the next change of duty station.

I was determined to submit my package for my master's in nursing. I loved how this specific degree dabbled into so many areas I loved, enjoyed, and was good at. I began that process, which consisted of continued classes, command involvement in the direction related to the degree, letters of recommendation, a clean officer record, good performance evaluations, passing my body composition test, and physical fitness test. So much pressure always rode on those last few.

Selected, was all I heard. I still feel it in my body today. A heart so full, a gasp of air as I yelped in excitement. The urge to call Keith and share our news that we would be leaving in a few months to California where his family lived. As I rushed up to my office to share with Rachel, my mentor, that I had been selected, I immediately worried if I was smart enough to achieve this. This was a great university and program. Smart people attended this college. *How was it I was selected?* I pivoted. *Candice, if you have proven anything to yourself over these last years, it is that you can do hard things. You are built to do hard things.*

Our favorite part of moving was the house search. Keith and I immediately started the process of discovering where we wanted to live, where the best schools were located, what made sense with my commute to school and Keith's commute to where he was going to be stationed. The excitement in the house was contagious; the Wests were headed west.

Maybe you, too, can relate to parts of this chapter—behaving in ways that felt misaligned to your core values, but are also a necessary means to cope with your surroundings. Perhaps looking back you can see circumstances where you deviated from your own personal truth to be accepted. That is the beauty in self-reflection and introspection—it serves as a permission slip to go within, to discover the deeply rooted beliefs that drive you to feel safety in all the above. To find safety outside of self. If this is you, I also see you. I witness your desire to feel safety, without judgment.

PERMISSION GRANTED to explore and heal from self-sabotage.

The Confrontation Era

*"Don't avoid conflict just to keep the peace.
You'll start a war within yourself instead."*

—Unknown

As I said in the beginning, this was my awakening era. I had just graduated from the university I was attending and was now living in a beautiful country overseas, having moved there from California.

This is where it all changed for me.

This is where I learned that what *you don't change, you choose*. And that *if you spot it, you got it*. Those were two key mottos I held close to me to help me on the road ahead. In the military we come from all walks in life... all cultures, ethnicities, belief systems, values, all of it. Then we are crammed into a general location and expected to thrive together as a unit, starting over every two to three years.

I always felt like I could sense things. Entering rooms, I would notice when there was tension or when it felt lighthearted and happy. I could read people, their body language, and really interpret their messaging before they spoke. And many times I didn't like the read I got. I felt like an outcast. I felt like I didn't belong. I could feel the fake smiles I received and could hear the whispers as I walked out of a room. I know I didn't fit the mold of the majority, and because of that, I wore masks to feel safe, secure, and a sense of belonging. At this point in my career, however, these masks were getting harder and harder to put on. I didn't know who I was supposed to show up as. To muddy the waters, I was also a rank. A rank that determined the level of responsibility, leadership, and authority I had governing staff I worked alongside with but also oversaw. When deep down you don't know who you are, and you add on multiple titles with varying expectations, the confusion is beyond comprehensible. Add on a life riddled in trauma and a fear of disappointing others, and it is the perfect recipe for a dysregulated nervous system.

As I worked through the varying areas identified through therapy and my life coach, essentially receiving support weekly alternating the two, I started to see exactly what they both spoke of. Being able to recognize where my mindset was driving my day to day gave me permission to slowly release the judgment I was serving myself, while also allowing me to practice reframing and applying what I was learning. I started seeing people I once respected and looked up to as extremely unhealthy for me, feeling disappointed that I hadn't seen it earlier. I recognized where the toxic was within me. Where I was the villain in the stories of those around me while also recognizing where I had been bullied, shamed, and discredited. Awareness is a beautiful thing, and it was in this awareness I gave myself permission to take back my personal power.

Part of taking back my personal power was confronting those who had taken bits and pieces of me along the way. For so many years, I felt so inferior when it came to me and how I measured up to my dad. I felt like I didn't matter. Like I wasn't good enough. Like he still held grudges from the past. When he drank it was always so much worse. But in this season of my life, I was tired of crying every time I watched a movie with a child and their father either in cahoots or forming a bond I knew I would never have. I was tired of being angry and holding a grudge

I was done. I was done letting life fly by me while I sat in the victim's seat. I made a decision that when I flew back to the United States to present at a conference, I would make the trip back to Ohio to have a conversation with my dad. I knew I needed to have a discussion with my father. I knew I needed to confront him about my childhood, to ask questions, gain clarity, and hear his explanation for how he treated me while under the influence. I knew I needed closure, and the only way to get it, and to understand his side, was to ask him.

Stepping onto the plane, one would think I would have been more nervous about my small presentation than a loving conversation with my dad. *Nope.* I had knots in my stomach the entire flight as I closed my eyes to see the stream of thoughts and questions I had for him just pop through, almost like text message bubbles. I tried to remain calm and not allow the mind to jump back into rabbit holes, reminding myself that between my therapy and life coaching calls, I was equipped.

I stayed with my sister Trichia. When I arrived, she opened her home to me and made me feel at home. She knew what was on the agenda, so I shared my plan. As I shared how nervous I was, how I feared his reaction, and even more, his response, I could feel my throat tighten. I knew, though, that I was in a stage in my healing that required this next step. This was pulling me down. It consumed way too much of my energy, and I could no longer allow the past to continue to steal my present and future.

I met up with my dad and stepmom, and we walked around the mall. I thought to myself, *I can't have this conversation here. The scene doesn't feel right.* Jennifer showed up with my niece and nephew and it sealed the deal—this conversation was not happening. After we walked around the mall we went to dinner, and I also received confirmation that this was not the time or place for a heavy discussion like this. The kids were loud, my sister was trying to keep them entertained, my dad looked like he was ready for his cocktails, and I began to think I was going to have to table it.

The next morning my dad and stepmom came to pick me up at Trichia's house, and we headed to a small cafe in downtown Norwalk. The town is small, so small the waitress behind the breakfast bar got to sit and hear the entire conversation; it was her lucky day. My dad, stepmom, and I sat down in this small cafe in the center of town, and I awkwardly viewed the menu, reading the same breakfast combo over and over. I remember the waitress coming to the table to take our order, and I immediately thought, *Oh, jeez, I haven't read past this first item. Guess that's what I will be ordering.* The waitress walked away, and we started some small talk. It was always awkward for me being with my dad. I only knew the intoxicated version of him because that is what was mostly present. I walked on eggshells around the sober dad. I never knew what was safe to say or not to say, and armored myself for criticism and judgment.

I knew I had to just rip off the Band-aid and start the conversation or it was never going to happen. I was in this energy of, *Am I avoiding it because I am fearful or am I avoiding it because I am being selfish?* Isn't it interesting how one can feel selfish, even for the slightest moment, for asking questions surrounding the abuse they endured? I counted down in my head, 3, 2, 1.....

"Hey Dad, I wanted to let you know I have been in therapy seeing a psychologist just trying to understand a little more about myself."

Giving me a blank stare while also nodding his head in approval, I shared with him that working with her and discovering lots about myself has led to questions. My dad continued to stare at me with a puzzled look on his face.

"Dad, I have a few questions I would like to ask to gain some closure."

As he was clearing his throat I was trembling in my chair. Armpits sweating, dry mouth, I wanted to just change the subject but I came here to do this; I'd made a commitment to myself and I was going to follow through. I would regret it otherwise. My stepmom sipped her coffee then stepped outside for a cigarette. That was when I got the nerve. Just a dad and his daughter.

Then suddenly the question fell out of my mouth: "Why did you let me live in the conditions I lived in? We were so poor, churches filling our pantry, Salvation Army Christmases, home infested with cockroaches. Dad, why was that okay with you? Why was that enough for me? Why didn't you take me?" Crying while simultaneously trying not to make a scene, I asked these questions, desperate for the answer that would make me feel complete. That would make all the pain go away.

"I didn't know it was that bad," he replied.

I continued sharing the abandonment I felt with tears streaming down my face. The lack of love I felt as his biological child.

At this point I could see the waitress behind the breakfast bar just staring and listening in like it was some reality television show. I felt vulnerable, exposed, selfish, and ashamed. *Did I truly have a reason to feel the way I did? Am I not considering his position? Am I supposed to be, as a child seeking closure?*

It was time to rip the second Band-aid off."Dad, I never felt like I mattered. You never took interest in anything I did. If it didn't have to do with sports, you didn't care. I loved theater, music, art, and you couldn't care less. Herbert was always the priority. It was always about him, which made me feel really small. I played in the pit orchestra for my musical, had a lead in the senior musical, and while I played sports and was terrible, I never felt the encouragement and support like you always had for Herbert. Why?"

I could see his eyes swell, but his face remained flat as he looked off into the distance. My dad knew sports. It was his passion, hobby, and something he was really good at. In my opinion, he gave it up to have a family. Because of that, he lived vicariously through the talent of Herbert, because sports was all he knew. But I just wanted to know that he was proud of me, too. That he could see me and my unique gifts. This segwayed into the very last piece I needed closure on. This seed had grown roots so deep it had overtaken the garden, it had overtaken me. I weed and weed, pull and pull, but it's so large and powerful it manages to keep growing. My hope and desire within my heart was that this conversation would help me, somehow, kill what has been growing within since age fifteen.

"My last question, Dad. Why did you feel the need to call me names all the time when you were drinking? So many nights a week I was shamed for being me. To prevent it from escalating, I had to leave the house, sometimes at 11 p.m., to walk up and down our street, hoping by the time I came back in you would be passed out sleeping. I didn't deserve it."

My dad sat there with the same flat affect, not saying a word. My stepmom came back in and joined us. She saw me in tears, my dad's blank face, and said, "Uh-oh." She quietly sat down and joined us. I continued sharing the mean things he said to me on repeat while I lived there: "You're a fat fuck, you're a beached whale, you are going to turn out to be just like your mom."

Sobbing while sharing those details and trying to catch my breath, I could see my stepmom just sitting there. Not that there was much she could do, but it certainly reminded me of all the times she just sat there during those late nights where I was being emotionally abused for being me. No support, nothing. Her silence in that very moment reminded me of her silence all those years. My dad sat in silence, too. I could see his eyes filled with tears, red, but also him holding his own. I asked one final time: "Why, Dad, why did I deserve this?"

"I don't remember any of it. I don't remember ever saying any of those things. I am sorry."

It was in that now moment it was all confirmed—he had been so drunk all those nights, year after year, he could never recall his actions and behaviors the next day. Some of his actions and behaviors planted deep seeds of *not enoughness* in my being, in my body, that would play out over every single relationship I would have in my life. He never knew the consequences of the abuse, because he never knew the abuse existed.

We headed back to my sister's house and you could hear a pin drop in the car. As he dropped me off knowing he wouldn't see me again for who knows how long, he stood in her driveway and wrapped his arms around me. I felt a sense of peace in that moment. My body was not rejecting his hug or his love. It was simply there, taking it all in.

I truly believe in my heart he had no idea of his behavior, or how much pain he caused me over the years. Like clockwork, he told me to have a safe flight back home and to let him know when I landed. It was a long trip back with a heavy heart and a troubled mind. I had closure, but there was a lot of healing left to do.

Just as I made it back safe and sound, I received a call from Jennifer. She shared how my dad called her informing her of our conversation. He alluded to me saying he was a bad father. Jennifer always does her best to remain neutral; it's something she has always been good about. She shared this with me not out of gossiping, but because she knew what I was working through and had been a supportive pillar through it all.

Immediately, I was upset. I could not believe he'd turned this private, vulnerable discussion into me blaming him for all my past mistakes and relationships. Nothing of the sort was even mentioned. I was immediately triggered, angered, and frustrated, and definitely felt misunderstood. It took so much courage for me to confront him, and I felt so disappointed he would act this way.

Now fully activated, from head to toe I felt rage. Hot, sweaty, I could talk a mile a minute, I was so furious. I reached out to my dad and shared my disgust at how he communicated our exchange in Ohio. I was so tired of the manipulation and keeping silent. We went back and forth, and it was in that moment I knew I could not continue down the path to healing while actively in contact with him. It was not healthy for me. I informed him that moving forward I would be disconnected from him. I shared that I needed to heal, and all this manipulation and chaos was not helpful. That was the start of our sixteen-month, no-contact relationship.

Boundaries are something I was not raised learning or enforcing. Having needs was not taught or even encouraged. In this chapter it took courage to seek clarity, understanding, and to set a boundary to put self-energy first. Maybe you can relate to pieces woven within. What difficult questions have you had to ask? What difficult questions have you had to answer? We live in a world where we get to live on both sides. Maybe not to the extremes here, but it exists. Be sure you witness yourself in this. There is a heaviness to boundaries when you were born and built having none. Know I see you in this; it gets easier.

PERMISSION GRANTED to confront your truths with courage and compassion.

The Self-Reclamation Era

"There is more wisdom in your body than in
your deepest philosophy."

—Friedrich Nietzsche

Navigating this new boundary with my father, I also moved through learning more about my physical body. It felt as if I had found a root. A root so deeply buried that as I pulled on it, it continued to unravel it was never ending. I pulled and pulled, unable to get to its bottom to expose the hate, anger, shame, sadness, grief, guilt, all the years of pent up and stored emotions and lived experiences. The more I tugged, bringing it to its surface, the more dirt and debris came up along with it. It felt like my physical body was falling apart, breaking and crumbling.

It was like my body gave up on me. It was as though it could no longer compensate for all I had been repressing, and what started off as a small tug on that root turned into something I could have never anticipated. I avoided it. I didn't want to feel it. I numbed myself daily with food and alcohol. Avoidance is denying and robbing yourself of a truth. And for me, I convinced myself and still believe a piece of the avoidance was consciously worrying about the unit staffing. But subconsciously, the avoidance was not wanting to feel to heal. I refused to relive some of these horrific experiences. I was scared. I was too stubborn.

Feeling, crying, sharing meant I was weak. So instead, self-soothing and numbing myself felt like the better option. That was until I landed myself in the emergency room for fellow peers and co-workers to tend to me.

Journal Entry

This vessel continues to carry me through it all.

But I see, know, and feel it's starting to get tired, my body that is.

I tear it down, I put it down, I shame it. I don't nourish it or move it.

It's now time I stepped up and took control ... it's held me, compensated for me, it's stepped up to the plate for me.

I no longer need that top cover.

I am strong, fierce, capable and able.

One morning before work I found myself feeling lightheaded and a woozy sensation overcome by body. I was escorted down to the ER from my unit to receive a workup—IV fluids and labs, which then resulted in having further testing—stool sample, anal exam, and a CT exam, all before 7:30 a.m. I sure know how to start a day! Then back to work I went. I was so humiliated and embarrassed because I knew better. I knew I should not have needed care; it was my own fault for not taking good care of my body. Aside from the workup, they also placed a referral for an EGD test due to my lab and stool sample results. Being overseas, I was referred to the host nation hospital where I was stationed and had the pleasure of being treated by their providers. They were accommodating and gentle. I would lie if I said I wasn't nervous—I couldn't understand a word they said, and here I was about to put a scope down my throat. I drifted off to sleep and woke to hear everything looked great, but they recommended a colonoscopy to see if the bleeding was coming from my lower gastrointestinal tract.

Because life just isn't simple, I was sent back to my OB/GYN for help with many months straight of bleeding and now passing large clots. As she did her exam, she noticed the pelvic organ prolapse she had diagnosed me with a year prior was getting worse. *Great!* I thought. She had a few suggestions, but being overseas we did not have pelvic floor physical therapy, so instead she referred me to a specialist in another location.

After some logistics and several months' notice, it was recommended I have surgery to fix my pelvic organ prolapse, insert mesh to fix my urinary incontinence, as well as have a partial hysterectomy. Oh, and while I was down there, since it would be for a couple weeks, to go ahead and have my colonoscopy. It is like my body had been trying to communicate to me for some time, although I lacked awareness to notice it, to hear it. It could no longer compensate. It could no longer keep quiet. It spoke to me the only way I would listen—by falling apart.

As I waited for the surgery day to approach, everything got worse: the pressure in my pelvic floor, the bleeding that led me to being so tired and unmotivated. I will never forget one morning before work as I got ready in the bathroom, feeling something heavy with lots of pressure below. I remember freaking out because I could poke and flick at something which I knew was not supposed to be there. *My insides are falling out,* I thought to myself. *What should I do?*

Will everything fall out? Why is it so rubbery? How do I put it back in there? So many questions ran through my head in that moment, wondering why in the hell my body was falling apart, literally.

I went into work, feeling pressure, walking with awkward strides, hustling to find my doctor. She was able to get me in before the clinic opened and performed an exam. "Candice, your bladder prolapsed!" she said as I lay there wondering what the fuck was happening. My bladder was in my vaginal canal trying to make a run for it. It clearly no longer felt welcomed. The doctor shared with me how, when this happens, I just shove it back in. Clean hands and a gentle push, and it will fit back in. I remember thinking, *Heck no! This is a definite no for me.* Sadness set in on that exam table. *I am not even forty years old and my pieces and parts are falling to bits.* I was devastated, sad, angry, and upset that I allowed this to happen because I was not taking care of myself. But I was now in a different energy. I was going to start getting healthy.

My father-in-law flew in to watch the three kids while Keith and I flew to another location for my surgery and colonoscopy. I had my first appointment to be evaluated by the specialist so he knew exactly what the surgery day would look like. During his exam he noted things were much worse than he had thought, given his dialogue with my provider. What was supposed to be a quick vaginal surgery to insert mesh, fix the prolapse, and conduct a partial hysterectomy was now going to be a ten-hour robotic abdominal surgery. I am sure you can imagine my reaction to the news. I knew it was all falling out, but I certainly did not expect to hear that. I had to make a decision so he could plan his team and get me booked for surgery on the day that alloted the time, resources, room, and robot. I knew it was time to put myself first. Keith was in agreement. My poor body had been talking to me for a few years, but I had ignored it. My now moment takeaway: *Your body is your permission slip. You just have to tuck away the ego so you can listen to it.*

I remember crying, wondering how on earth I was not even forty and this was happening. My poor body. *How have I not taken care of it? How have I disregarded and ignored it?* This sacred vessel of mine, always showing up for me. Honest in all its forms. Truthful in its representation of my efforts. Loyal in the way in which it communicates to me. Strong as it has carried me through so much in just this lifetime. Compassionate in that it continues compensating, even through repeated self-sabotage.

I have believed, since starting my healing journey, that we cannot control how we were raised. But once we have awareness of patterns, themes, shadows, and trauma, it is our responsibility to ourselves and those we surround ourselves with to do *the work* to heal. We cannot live our lives blaming our parents or others who have harmed us or done us wrong. There is a strong difference in identifying with being a victim and living in victim energy. I love these quotes by Carl Jung as they speak exactly to this: *"Until you make the unconscious conscious, it will direct your life and you will call it fate,"* and *"I am not what happened to me. I am what I choose to become."*

I stepped into the gastrointestinal clinic the morning of my colonoscopy, having almost shit myself numerous times on the way there. I literally took a hotel hand towel and placed it between my legs as a handmade diaper on the way to the hospital in the event my sphincter gave out. Let's face it: three kids, a pelvic organ prolapse, coupled with irritable bowel syndrome and nerves was a perfect recipe for a mess.

I got called back and everything moved rather quickly. I remember lying on my left side, the beeping of the machines, large monitors on the wall, the coolness of the room, and so many people. And then it was like the lights went out. Before I knew it I was waking back up and conveniently farting all at the same time. Nothing says *Candice is alive and well* quite like that. I was informed they had found two large polyps, large enough that they required *piece-milling* to be removed and that they tattooed the spaces for my follow-ups for easy identification to check there is no re-growth. I felt full gratitude for the removal as they ended up being pre-cancerous. A full gratitude moment for listening to my body, for not dismissing her and her communication like I had over the years, and a full gratitude moment for me choosing myself and standing up for myself when I was told this request was not warranted.

I was finally listening to her. My sacred vessel. My intuition. And she hadn't steered me wrong. I reflected over the next couple days before my big surgery. The instance where I almost passed out leading me to the emergency room, the blood in the stool, then the hospital where my EGD was perfect, to a colonoscopy finding something that would have literally gutted me: it was the permission slip I needed to continue tuning into her. It was the permission slip I needed to start putting myself in the driver seat. It was the permission slip I needed to realize that this mission I was on, this mission of proving my worth, was, in fact, killing me slowly.

Surgery day arrived, and I was so nervous. Definitely had the shits, fear, worry, anxiety… all of it was bubbling to the surface. But God had truly brought me the exact professionals I needed for this journey. I felt so grateful as I lay there staring at all the bright lights and listening to the commotion of everyone preparing to dissect and repair my entire abdominal and reproductive cavity.

I woke up with thirteen new incisions on my abdomen and pelvic region, two of which were a result of the drilling through my pelvic bone that needed to take place for certain devices and mesh to be placed properly. Initially I was comfortable. I was tolerating the medication, fluids, and light foods. I remember seeing myself and being sad that *this was almost 40*. I was determined to continue being strong. But with addiction so rampant in my family line, strong in this case meant suffering through pain. Keith was amazing at waking me and giving me meds. He created multiple alarms on his phone so he knew which I was due for. I was so grateful for his help and support. We worked really hard together, checking all the boxes to avoid post-operative complications, but I was so headstrong that I was suffering in other ways.

I remember going to my seven-day follow-up appointment and the doctor being stern with me because I was not taking the pain medications often enough or in the correct dose. I was so fearful of getting hooked, and I wanted to make sure I had enough to last me throughout my long flight back home. The doctor and Keith reminded me of the process and how pain medications actually work. I remember telling myself quietly inside my head how I knew this, but I couldn't quite understand why there was this barrier preventing me from making myself feel comfortable. I had to remind myself by looking in the mirror and visually seeing all the scars, swelling, and bruising that my pain was not my imagination, but my reality. And another reminder to myself that I am not my parents. I didn't realize how much I feared becoming an addict and how deeply rooted in me it was.

Our flight back was long but comfortable. We returned home, and I had to constantly remind myself of my physical limitations. It was so hard to allow everyone to take care of me while I just sat and did nothing. I felt helpless. But it was that or risk damaging and tearing all the reconstruction. And there it was, the next layer of my healing revealed.

As I sat in my recliner couch watching my kids doing TikTok dances off of YouTube since school was no longer in-person, I tried to find myself in the energy of acceptance and also gratitude. Acceptance that I was home recovering and there was nothing I could do to support my unit during this pandemic. Acceptance that this time was for me to truly heal. It was a test of how much I was willing to listen, to surrender. How much I would try to cut corners to people-please. How I would shame and guilt myself into finding a way from home to help with the chaos at work. How willing I was to put myself first.

This was the next weed that needed to be pulled. It was not enough that I left for two weeks of testing, surgery, and post-operative recovery. But now I was back for eight weeks of convalescent leave to fully recover during a pandemic that left my unit extremely short-staffed. And with the ever-changing data and information that came out, I knew this was right up my alley given my specialty and expertise. But, even more, it was my test of how much I valued myself. How much I was willing to put myself first. How much I was willing to quiet the ego so I could listen to my body, nourish my body, and give it what it needed.

For those of you like me, you know the deep anguish you feel when you cannot be counted on or relied on. You consider it a flaw when you have to say no and are unable to make something work. You feel helpless when you are needed and not available. Every time my phone buzzed, whether through a text message, phone call, or a notification from our unit's chat string, it felt like an electric jolt through my entire body. Heart racing and palpating … fear. Fear of what they thought of me.

Reader, here is your permission slip to circle back to self. To schedule your screenings. To see the doctor. To quiet the ego and the noise. To put down the to-do lists and instead sit in stillness, feeling the sensations of your physical body. Get to know this sacred vessel. This sacred vessel carrying you through it all has a message for you. Only you cannot hear it on your calls, in your meetings, while driving your kids from karate to basketball. It is a sacred practice, one that will give you all the answers you need. So I challenge you to build a daily practice of tuning into self, to listening to the wisdom from within.

PERMISSION GRANTED to reconnect with and honor the wisdom of your body.

The Crossroads Era

"Caught between a strong mind and a fragile heart."

—Unknown

Moving through the next couple months in chaos between the pandemic, recovering from surgery, and preparing for our move back to the United States, I learned my dad was ill with cirrhosis of the liver. Over the next couple months, my stepmom provided updates from doctors, lab results, and other key details to keep me informed. I shared what I knew from a nursing perspective, having cared for patients like this before. According to family members I did speak with, dad was in denial. No longer drinking, he thought he would get better and that his condition would reverse. He thought he would be eligible for a transplant.

Father's Day approached, and I was just not in a place to reach out. We had not been talking, and he had shared his desire with family that I was not to know about his illness, so I thought, *Why bother?* After so many talks and arguments throughout my lifespan with him surrounding his alcohol consumption, I was hurt and angry. Even though I knew and understood why, it still made me feel like I was not good enough. That us kids, the grandkids, that all our love for him was just not enough. That we were not enough to fight for. Clearly I was circling in the victim energy, making it about me.

We finally got the green light to move back to the West Coast after three years overseas and arrived safe and sound. What an adventure returning with all five of us, our two cats, and what felt like a billion pieces of luggage to the Navy Lodge where we would remain in quarantine for fourteen days before reporting to our new duty station. We had two rooms; I shared a room with Nattie, and Keith was with the boys. Nattie's eighteenth birthday was the day after we arrived. We did our best to celebrate her, but it was hard being confined to a hotel room. We kept busy with TV, and Nattie even took the extra time to study for her driver's test. We found ways to keep occupied and appreciated the down time to adjust back to our new time zone and just relax.

And just when we were catching our breath from the hustle and bustle of what felt like the last three years straight, I received a text message from Herbert. They were estimating as best as they could given my dad's condition, but he was being placed on hospice and I was told he had maybe a week left. I was still in quarantine, barely checked into my command, but now needing to take emergency leave. What a mess. I felt so confused, it was like a ball was sitting in my gut. If I stayed behind out of fear, I would miss saying goodbye and likely live in regret. If I went and managed to catch something and spread it to those who had weakened immune systems, I would also feel horrible. I really had to weigh my options. At the time so much fear was being projected from news outlets, social media platforms, and people, I didn't know what to do or believe.

My life was rooted in fear, in case you haven't noticed this pattern.

I reached out to Jen, my life coach, to talk this through, because I knew there were no take-backs. I either went or I didn't. I also wanted to consider my dad and his wishes since we were not on speaking terms. *Did he even want me there?* I called my stepmom to ask if I should come. I shared with her my concerns regarding wanting him to remain peaceful as he made his transition. She replied, "He would really like you to be here. He has some things he would like to clear his conscience of, and some things he would like to say to you." I was surprised to hear that, to be honest. I knew I needed to put my fear aside and make the trip. He needed this. I needed this. We needed this.

I arrived in South Carolina, deplaned, got my luggage, and met Herbert. I got into the car and we started to drive off. Suddenly my brother pulled off to the side, still at the airport, got out of his car and jogged over to the porta potty set out for the construction workers. As I sat there laughing at him, next thing I saw was the door of the porta potty swinging open. The door hadn't sealed all the way and he was literally standing there using the restroom with the world watching as they drove by. It was the full-body giggle laugh I needed in that now moment. As much as my siblings and I are all different, we are the same.

Not long after getting settled in and catching up, it was shared with me that my stepmom felt my father's current state was my fault. It was stated, "If Candice would have just shut her mouth we wouldn't be in this situation. Why did she have to bring all that up? Things were fine." Apparently the cafe chat in Ohio before I went no-contact triggered him to stop drinking briefly. Once that short window was over he returned to his daily drinking, but apparently increased the amount he was drinking. This pushed him into his diagnosis shortly after the new year.

I remember hearing that and being in shock. I just couldn't comprehend how I was being targeted as the problem. Just another reminder that I am *too much*, it is not safe to *speak my truth*, I talk *too much*, I am *too opinionated*, and I am *heavily misunderstood*.

My stepmom, I believe, was in pain. Blaming me likely felt easier than truly looking at the entire situation at face value. Because in reality, it wasn't her fault either. My father abused alcohol—it was on him, and him only. I made the decision in that moment to tuck all those feelings into a place in my body and move on. I was there to give and find closure. That evening I spent with the family just reflecting on how we all got where we were. *How was I at my brothers in July awaiting my fathers demise?* It all felt so weird, and also like I always knew this would be the case.

The next day we all headed over to my dad's house. I felt uncomfortable; I didn't know what to expect from everyone, including Dad. I didn't know how my presence would be received, even though I was told he wanted me there. At the first glimpse of him, I was in shock: skinny, frail, yellow, bruising on his arms, and the roundness of his stomach from his ascites. Even though my brother tried preparing me with pictures, seeing him in person was so different.

At first glance I looked away, aware my facial expressions gave away my thoughts. I didn't want to stare. I didn't want him to feel bad about himself. He knew how he looked—it was hard to even notice it was him. I could sense his discomfort, though he appeared happy and sparked up conversations with us. Talking felt awkward, but it was even more awkward sitting and staring in silence. My stepmom was in the kitchen making lunch for us all, and the nieces and nephews were all running around playing. I was observing. I was listening to the exchanges, taking pictures of interactions, and feeling sadness that this was the first time in so many years we were all together. *Why is that? Why is it that funerals and weddings are the events where people all come together to witness one another, celebrate life, and catch up?* Life gets so busy, and in the blink of an eye we are all grown, raising our own families, and asking ourselves where all the time went.

In the early afternoon, hospice came by. They were doing their daily assessment, reviewing medications for comfort, and met the entire crew there by dad's side. It was hard to separate the nurse in me and to just show up as the daughter, which is what was requested. Dad shared bits and pieces of us all with the hospice team, acknowledging things we had done. I think it was his way of sharing how proud of us he was. He pointed out my flag I had flown over a specific area overseas, while deployed. "That's Candice— she's the one in the Navy that deployed," he said. It felt as if he had spoken of me before and was trying to connect the dots for the hospice nurses. Deep down I believe he was proud of me, but not hearing it sober made it hard to hear those words over all the bad ones for all those years. I appreciated his effort and offered back a gentle smile.

It was a good day. We shared stories, caught up on life, and I got to meet my niece and nephew for the first time. It felt good to be in the present moment taking in all these last memories with Dad. I planted seeds of gratitude, forgiveness, and compassion.

We went back to my brother's house and we all unwound from the heaviness of the day. The truth was, we were all there because death was upon us. As much as we laughed and smiled throughout the day, there was a murkiness just underneath the surface. It was when we got home that we could feel that, or at least I could. I remember going to sleep that night feeling some heaviness I couldn't identify—unsure if it were regret for the no-contact, anger for his self-inflicted circumstances, or just my life in general all coming to a head.

The next day, just as we were ready to head over to my dad's, Herbert received a call from my stepmom that my dad was not feeling well. He'd had a difficult night. He had been throwing up blood, was in lots of pain, and was having difficulty even moving. They said they were going to head to the hospital to be evaluated. Hours later we heard back that he would require admittance to the hospital. As a nurse, the writing was on the wall. I knew exactly what was happening, and it was so hard to hear the opinions of others regarding next steps when I knew he was deteriorating. I knew we were at the point of no return, and all we could do was make him comfortable and ensure he was not alone.

Hospice arrived shortly after he came home. He was trying to put on a strong face, but I could see right through it. *I am he, he is me.*

We all realized this rapid decline overnight was just the beginning. I knew from past experience, working in nursing homes and at the hospital for so many years, that in the death and dying process one will get a surge of energy. It almost looks as if they are making a turn for the better, but really, it is them soaking in the last of their time left on earth. Capturing the final memories! It is, unknowingly, their gift to their family: the last smiles, the last laughs, the last stories, the last of what needs to be said. Knowing this was likely why he presented as he did yesterday, we all decided it was probably a good time to have our final conversations with him while he was still coherent.

We all stayed outside so we each had privacy to share intimately and honestly, and just be at his bedside. It was heartbreaking watching family come and go. We all knew our own individual relationships with him, but we also had an idea of each others' from our own personal lens and observations. I found myself offering for others to go ahead of me. Jennifer and her son would be leaving before me, so she of course had to go first. Elise... well, she needed closure, too, so I offered her to go ahead of me. Herbert, Eileen, my uncle... I always disappeared when it came time to swap out. They needed it more than me. It was the story I was sticking to because I didn't know what to say to him. I felt like I'd let him down. I felt like I'd abandoned him. I felt guilt and shame for putting myself first *and* trying to heal in order not to become him.

It was getting late, and the family started to head out for the night so Dad could get some rest. We all said our goodbye to him one by one giving our hugs and kisses, because his decline was so rapid from the day prior none of us knew what to expect by morning. There I was. Walking into the living room as he stared at the television and watched the Cubs game.

"Hey Dadeo, who is winning?" I asked him with a smile on my face and a subtle laughter in my tone. He had his typical witty response, "Not the Cubs, and they won't unless they get their heads out of their asses." I chuckled, he chuckled, and then I told him I would be back tomorrow and that I expected him to tell me who won the game.

As I turned around to walk out of the living room I heard, "Candice?"

"Yeah Dad," I replied.

"I love you," he said.

"I love you too, Dad."

I knew this was the last time I would ever hear those words from his mouth. I hear them right now as I share this. A softness in his voice, a delivery of deep sorrow, remorse, and tender love he'd never shown me. People underestimate the power of words, their delivery and their tone. Words have such power, and we often don't realize their effect until much too late. I walked out making every attempt to keep it together. I took all I was feeling and tucked it into another part of my body.

As we wound down for bed, my sister and I lay on the bed chatting about the day. Suddenly, the ceiling got my attention. I could see things moving in the air above me. They were moving in a circular motion, and it was quite alarming and noticeable.

"Jennifer, do you see that? Do you see that swirling on the ceiling?" I asked.

"I don't see a thing," she shared.

Standing up, I tried to grab at it or touch it, but my hand would just go through it.

"You're scaring me, Candice. I don't see anything. I am straining my eyeballs trying to see something, but nothing is there," chuckled Jennifer.

I told her how it didn't feel scary at all. It felt so peaceful and it felt safe. We laughed so hard. It didn't make sense at all. How was I seeing this swirly circling thing above us, but she couldn't see anything? We knew it was time to get some rest, so as she drifted off to sleep, I just laid there noticing what was above me. And in true Candice fashion, I tried to make sense of it all and figure out what it was. This was just another *thing* that I added to my list of experiences.

Morning was here before I knew it. I felt like I had just fallen asleep. It was an active night of dreams and I just didn't feel as rested as I would have liked. We all headed over to my dad's house early in the morning as my sister had to head back to Ohio. When we arrived, his condition had not improved at all. He did appear to be more comfortable; I credit that to his pain medications. He was sitting up in his chair, and he tried so hard to be able to find the strength to stand on his own to hug Jennifer goodbye. He just didn't have it in him.

As the day continued on, he appeared increasingly uncomfortable. We helped him to his bed, making sure to rotate him every couple hours, talked with him, and held his hand as he drifted back and forth from being awake to a deep sleep. We spent time at his side just being present with him so he knew that he was not alone. Looking at his frail body taken over by this illness, the yellow on his skin, the sunken eyes, skin tears and bruising, I knew when I left it was soon. I felt it to my core.

Herbert and I decided to head out for the night. We knew we needed the rest, as it had been so emotionally taxing. My brother was not one to show emotion, but I could see him carrying a heaviness he didn't know what to do with. I remember on the car ride home seeing the same numbers on the clock, radio station, and road sign. It was so synchronistic as it was right after the thought crossed my mind that he would pass the following day. I thought to myself, *What the fuck? What does that mean? Does that mean I am right?* Oh boy, that sat with me for a minute. I got so curious wondering what those numbers represented. Many would say… the time, radio station, and route you're on. But I knew better. There had been way too many things happening over the last few days to discount that they held a greater purpose and meaning. I sat staring out the window in deep reflection of how the trip had been going so far. I kept thinking about the conversation of how Dad wanted to clear his conscience. In his current state, I knew that was not going to happen. I'd kept encouraging everyone to have their closure with him ahead of me, but now my closure was never going to happen.

We finally arrived back at my brother's. As we went inside, we quite literally sighed simultaneously as we exhaled deeply. We chatted about Dad's presentation and how we knew death was knocking at his door. We chatted about how we felt everyone else was holding up, predicting what tomorrow would bring, and then we received a call. It was my stepmom. Dad was now making rattling noises as he breathed. From my experience in this field, one usually passes within twenty-four hours once the *death rattle* starts. We talked about how we would rotate to help so she wasn't having to stay up all night and then the following day. We headed to bed so we could get some sleep before we needed to head back out.

As if things hadn't already been strange for me, I laid down and the most wild thing happened. I was starting to think I was sleep deprived. I said my prayers as I closed my eyes. I asked for all the protection, strength, wisdom, and for my dad to be comfortable and at peace. Shortly afterwards, I drifted off to sleep, so I thought, and suddenly

I was visualizing images in my mind. But it felt so real and like I was awake. What I saw was an old school projector with numerous photos flipping so fast I could hardly make out what they were. But there were so many pictures of my dad. Pictures of all of us together. Old pictures, new pictures. These pictures were memories—some I could instantly recognize, others not so much. Opening my eyes, freaked the hell out and wondering what all this meant, I thought, *Is this my dad's life in review?* I once was told that as people pass on they spend time reviewing their life and the impact they made, could have made, and where their actions had positive and less than desirable effects. *Is there truth to that?* I have no clue. But what I could gather from that experience was confirmation of my earlier thoughts, and the synchronistic numbers that followed. I was surprised by my composure. This was definitely something new to me. I was having all sorts of wild dreams, visions, and experiences, and aside from Eileen, I was keeping this information close to myself.

The next morning, Herbert and I met downstairs to start our drive back to my dad's. We got there, came inside, and saw Dad resting. He was shutting down. I felt sadness but also hated seeing him this way, so I knew that the end result was much better than this now moment and the ones that immediately followed. I felt angry with myself for not having my closure with him. I was angry with myself for not being brave enough to start the conversation with him. I just didn't know how to talk to him. I just didn't know what to say. *Would I say something wrong that would upset him?* Because that was our history… my questions, words, thoughts, all of it triggered him. I didn't want him triggered in his final days. I didn't want to be the cause of any extra stress or discomfort. Bottom line, we didn't know one another, and that made it hard for us. And as much as we were so very different, we were so very much alike.

My stepmom had music playing in the background, which had such a calming effect. It felt so peaceful in the space. Though peaceful, we felt we needed to shift gears a bit to liven up the energy in the room. Jimmy Buffet and REO Speedwagon were hands down what we needed in that now moment. It was perfect. We all chuckled, laughed, and sang as Dad slept peacefully. I happened to look up in laughter and in that now moment noticed the title of the song: "Between Two Worlds." I jumped up in urgency moving to Dad's side. I grabbed his hand. I knew that hidden message, what it meant, and I was not second guessing what my body felt. I felt for a pulse, noticing it was weak and slow. I told Herbert and Elise to get my stepmom, that it was time; I had a deep knowing.

All of us surrounded his bedside. We told him we would be fine, that he could go if he was ready. And within seven minutes from that sign I received through music, he took his last breath. We could all hear life leave his physical body. I felt numb, maybe even dissociated. It felt like I could not feel what I needed to, and it felt like I was at peace. It was a weird dance between the two.

The next morning we headed to the funeral home to discuss his cremation and finalize all the details. From there, I headed straight to the airport, since I was closing on our house later that day. Phew! Walking through the airport almost like a mummy, zoned out, blank stare, I stopped to grab a water and snack for the flight, then headed to the bathroom and finally my gate. It was time to board. As I grabbed my phone to pull up my boarding pass, I realized I didn't have it. Frantically retracing my steps, I rushed back to where I'd bought the water. The lady at the checkout held up my phone asking, *"Are you back for this?"* She smiled, but in that moment I got this feeling. Her eyes… there was something about her eyes. Call me crazy, but it felt like it was my dad. I felt like he was staring directly into my soul, showing me he was still here and still protecting me. My mentor had told me she felt my dad and I would have a better relationship in his afterlife than we ever could have had while he was here in the physical world. I believed that fully as I sat in deep reflection.

The duality of death, both painful and beautiful. Maybe you, Reader, have lost someone close to you. What would you give to have moments to share in a story, offer appreciation of their impact on your life, or maybe to express the pain you've felt in its place? Know there is no right or wrong—it all just is. I encourage you to connect to self and discover what it is you need for closure. At times what we think we need is not, in fact, what we need. Get out of your head, and instead, connect with your heart. What do the beats whisper? What is it you really need in these now moments to feel complete, to feel closure? The answer is within.

PERMISSION GRANTED to embrace your journey and find your own path to peace.

The Spiritual Era

"Spirituality does not come from religion. It comes from our soul."

—Anthony Douglas Williams

It felt like a long flight home. I landed, and Keith greeted me at curbside pickup, placing my luggage in the trunk of the car. As we drove off, he asked the expected question: "How are you?" Then, I said I was fine, but now I realize I was dissociating to avoid actually having to feel. Dad and I never got the closure we both desired.

Keith and I headed back, discussing what the next few days would bring. We headed to the closing office to sign the documents for our new home. On the to-do list we had to purchase new vehicles and furniture, enroll the kids in school, schedule medical and dental appointments, check into our new command, and hit the ground running with rank performance evaluations shortly after arriving. There was a giant list I got to immerse myself into to avoid feeling it all. Just another period of my life where I tucked it all away somewhere inside the body, knowing it would hold me.

Those initial months were hard. Keith and I both worked full time without tele-working privileges. The pandemic was still very much in its heightened stages so we felt locked in our home. The kids were doing virtual school at home, with Keith's mom, Gigi, living with us and supervising. Nattie did a full pivot and pulled out of college to stay home, attend community college, and work full time. Things were so chaotic. All the adults coped through drinking and drunchies (drunk and munchies), the kids immersed themselves in video games, and Nattie shopped and swiped right trying to meet people her age. In just a matter of a few months, *July through October:*

- We moved overseas then back to the West Coast.
- My father died.
- We closed on our home.
- We received and unpacked two shipments of household goods.
- We enrolled the kids in school and medical/dental care.
- We purchased new cars.
- Gigi lived with us.
- My mother had health issues.
- One of our children was diagnosed with level two autism.

Gulp, deep breath… it became so heavy. And as if there wasn't enough going on, I was also considering how I was going to transition from active duty to retirement life in three years, what interested me, and the direction I felt called to. So as if my plate wasn't full enough, I enrolled in what came to be a three-year life coaching academy with Nancy Levin, best selling author and Master Life Coach. Keith was supportive of this—he knew I was deep in my healing and had a desire to help others, and this could be a great way to transition myself into military retirement while earning an income. It felt like perfect timing to start preparing.

As I started to get settled into the new duty station, I quickly shifted my approach from an overachieving, boundaryless, people-pleasing go-getter to someone deeply rooted in efficiency and family life. I found going to work at the time I needed to and leaving right on time without an ounce of guilt. *This was new for me.* In all the years I'd served, I was typically one of the very first in and one of the last to leave.

Having experienced boundaries for the first time, I was in awe that so many people lived this way all the time. This was a new concept for me that left me completely speechless. It also brought a newfound awareness to the actions of other people whose paths I crossed along the years. I used to find myself labeling people as lazy or not team oriented, but now I found myself questioning if they just had boundaries. I questioned why I had been this way throughout my whole career. It didn't take long for me to learn and recognize through the coaching program that all of this work I had put forth all of the years—all of the time and the energy and the to-do lists—all of it were just ways to prove my own worth to myself. By being selected for the hard jobs, the high visibility collaterals, getting the early promotion on my personal evaluation, it all meant I was worthy, valued, accepted … *and that I mattered.*

I finally got to the point where, when I was on leave, I didn't answer my phone or emails. I can't remember the last time that was ever the case. To me, not being accessible on vacation meant I was not committed, dependable, or a dedicated team player… a warped thought process, I know! I found myself informing bosses of appointments versus asking to be excused. I found myself working alongside everyone versus working for myself. It truly changed the dynamic and what I was able to experience.

And as if the timing couldn't have been any better, as I was releasing my attachment to my job, producing outcomes, and being the go-to sailor, my home life was in shambles. Since my dad had passed away, I had definitely started experiencing things I hadn't routinely before. As I mentioned before, things started happening during my travels down to see my dad and then throughout my stay there in South Carolina. But once I got back, even more started happening. I believe I merged these experiences and my dad dying together, creating these thoughts in my mind that my dad was connecting with me beyond the physical plane. This made me feel connected to him, it made me feel like he was still there with me, and I thought it was his way of showing me how much he loved me. Remember, we didn't get that closure. We didn't get to have that conversation. So I felt in my heart like this was his way of connecting with me beyond the grave. And to be honest, God felt obsolete. *Why would he allow any of this to happen?* My entire life had been one trainwreck after another. Pain and more pain. A loving God wouldn't do this to people. A good God wouldn't allow people to continuously suffer over and over again. I was absolutely done with him. My thoughts … *who fucking cares about going to hell? I am currently living in it.*

I remember as a little girl always having the ability to see things. I remember as a little girl going places, staying at friend's houses, babysitting, and always just feeling a presence even though nothing was there physically. A lot of times, honestly, I thought I was crazy and paranoid. I remember the first home I purchased, Nattie being very young, and while I was giving her a bath the downstairs TV came on. There was no other explanation other than some kind of ghostly spirit hanging out in the house with us. I would go to sleep at night and just feel this cool breeze with the gentle pressure over me, and then it would just go away. But I always got this feeling that there was something there. While living overseas I would see dark movement in my bedroom, and it used to freak me out. I would wake Keith up, asking him, "Do you see this? I see it again, it's moving in the room." I just knew he thought I was nuts. This stuff just kept happening, but it amplified even more after my dad passed.

Diving into the New Age healing that seemed to become a trend all over socials, I got curious. I believed to the depth of my soul that it was my father trying to help me heal all my pain. It is what introduced me to holistic healing. I started educating myself and learning more about the body on a metaphysical level. Learning about energy, chakras, and how the body really does hold the repressed and suppressed. It all started making sense to me from a physical standpoint. I started weaving together my health ailments from a small child to this current now moment, seeing how my physical body had been trying to communicate with me this whole time. I became obsessed with learning, something I didn't learn until later on was a big issue for Keith. He never spoke up; instead, he kept supporting me, but also building more and more resentment.

I started to really understand the depth of the physical body and how much we didn't know. I joined program upon program because I was so curious and wanted to learn it all. One particular program I joined turned out to be something a little darker than my liking. I started noticing even more things that spooked me while in that course, so much so that I didn't complete it. I was not one to quit something, but for me, the writing was on the wall. I started wondering if this line of work was for me. I really struggled with this. Part of me felt it was my dad, part of me felt like it was darkness, part of me felt like I was overthinking it all. I often denied my own intuition, and for as long as I can remember I operated off of self-doubt over self-trust. I truly believed in angels, I knew that to be certain. I just felt such internal conflict and tried to figure out what was spiritually real.

I had started to receive some very pointed and specific downloads of something that seemed very healing for myself and could be useful for others. Again, I felt it was a gift from my dad. Keeping it close, I ventured off to my very first retreat in Binghamton, New York, where a beautiful friend, Michelle, would be hosting. I had the most amazing experience. Throughout my time there, more and more understanding popped in. We had a group healing session where it was like I had drifted off into another world. Lying on my back, close by the boat dock, the sound of water, birds, and crystal singing bowls humming, I tuned into self. Shutting off the outside world, noise, and chaos of it all, I welcomed the peacefulness I felt. I was flooded with warmth, then a coolness from head to toe, and back to internal heat, and my mind was still. I saw colors swirling around in my mind's eye, so many variations of the same color. It actually reminded me of the aurora borealis. As I allowed myself to be swept away in the moment, fully connected to self, I heard it so clearly: "It is not your fault." Still in this in-between state, tears fell down the sides of my face. Allowing myself to remain in the stillness and my mind off, I allowed the experience to unfold. I remember feeling peace and gratitude. It was such a release. Then my mind was activated and took charge. *Which part? Which part is not my fault, I need to know!* Was it me getting kicked out at fifteen, lying to the police because I was scared, the miscarriage, my father's death? *Which of all of this was not my fault? Which story are you giving me permission to let go of? Which story can I close and put on the shelf and no longer open or read again? Which root can I pull and no longer water?* I needed more, and I got what I needed, not what I wanted.

Before even fully returning home from the weekend event, I was woken many nights from sleep with clear messages that I would document in detail. And that is where I developed my Just PIVOT five-step mindset tool. I started to see my work as a way to help others pivot—shifting from their current spiral and trigger, getting to the root, and reframing to a healthier place and state of being. I was in such gratitude and started to see that God and spirituality co-existed. *Why is it this or that, why not both?*

I continued exploring and just really being excited about the things I was creating. This was new to me, *but was it really?* You see, for years I had been in the energy of creation at work—programs, educational material, workshops, and planning celebratory events. This was the same thing, but just for a different purpose. I quickly realized that I had been doing this work all along.

As I dove into this work I grew to love so much, I was receiving so much judgment and hate from those who identified themselves as religious. Had I been creating biblical affirmation cards or journals, it would have been widely accepted. So many with the *come one, come all* vibe encouraged me to shift out of the New Age spirituality and believe in God. But then they'd say in the next breath, "But only if you don't ____, ____, ____ ." The people telling me Jesus, God, and the Bible were the only way and to follow his Word were also the most judgmental to those of us confused or having our own belief system. *Why on earth would I want to subscribe to all that?* I thought. It certainly didn't feel like a *come one, come all, come as you are* invitation. It felt like judgment, a *come only if you are like us* invitation. No one seemed to want to offer education or have a meaningful conversation about it—they just wanted to tell us we were going to hell. What many of them didn't realize is that we already felt like we were living in it and had been our whole life. It made me even more resistant, pushing me even further away from it all.

Jen, my mentor, and I would have deep conversations about this because I was so confused. I thought I believed in God. I felt like I did. I had felt his hand in my life so many times through turbulent times, but now I was just down right angry with him and exiled him. I clung to the New Age spirituality because I felt connected to it. I felt my father. And, I needed him to heal the guilt I felt. Deep down I felt like it was my fault. I allowed the words of others and the planting of this seed to take root. Even though my family members told me it wasn't my fault, the fact my stepmom allegedly told others it was didn't sit well with me. It was exactly what I needed to hear and believe to reinforce the childhood story of, I am a *bad person*. I owned it, carried it, and watered it. I allowed it to overgrow and consume a part of me. So if this was my dad trying to guide and direct me to heal, then so be it. It was symbolic in that he forgave me, he didn't see it as my fault. Now he was trying to help me see that.

As I learned new modalities, I started to see exactly what was for me and what was not. I totally believe in energy and the storage within the body. I totally believe we are surrounded by earth angels helping guide us. I believe our ancestors are always here cheering us on in the background, waiting for us to ask them for guidance and support. And signs, I believe in signs. Those are everywhere if you're willing to pay attention. *I mean, why would I not believe them?* Just before my dad passed, reading the song title on the TV is what directed me to his bedside. I can't imagine a more beautiful way to support him as he transitioned. And before his passing, seeing the projector visualization served as information to me that he would be transitioning soon.

Then the reiki. I received so much judgment from others for learning this modality. It was founded in Japan many years ago, and has helped so many people with chronic pain, stress, and feelings of anxiety. Honestly, what is the difference between someone bowing and praying and experiencing "miracle" healing and reiki, where hands are hovered or a distant intention is set and then someone has improved wellness or is healed? The more judgment I received, the more I felt religion and God were a lie. No longer believing in any of that while also confused with spirituality, I felt overwhelmed.

I slowly deciphered what modalities felt aligned and which ones were just a hard no. But I knew I needed to do this on my own. I couldn't do it with *religious* people spewing judgment and hatred down my hatch, being the complete opposite of what they preached. But it was like the stars aligned. After months of feeling a numbness in my body from God, spirituality, all these New Age modalities, I just wanted to burn it all down. I felt like my head was going to explode. It's truly hard to describe how on edge and discombobulated I felt. One breath, I shamed myself and the thousands of dollars spent to learn it all. Another breath was the time spent away from family to learn it all. Then another breath worrying what I would do when I retired. The cycle of overthinking and overanalyzing everything was absolutely paralyzing. I didn't know what to believe. I didn't feel like I could trust my intuition. I was completely fearful that I was going to do something wrong and truly end up in hell. What kind of spirituality, God, or New Age places this kind of fear in someone? You don't follow the Bible to a tee? You're outcast and going to hell. New Age practices? You're going to hell. *How does one decide for self what is best? How does one go through life experiencing what works for them and what feels good for them with overhanging fear?* I began to feel like I was damned if I do, damned if I don't.

With everything else that was going on I just wanted to burn it down. I didn't know what I believed anymore. Keith had his own personal religious trauma, so he also had exiled God and wasn't someone unbiased I could speak with. He also did not understand what I was doing, so even though I vented, he didn't know how to offer support. I was happy with the simple fact he listened. Bottom line, I wasn't trusting myself.

I relied heavily on my mentor for this topic. I found myself using her ears as a way to be able to fully express my thoughts and really sort them out, and to share my confusion and misunderstandings of all the different practices and judgments that came along with them all. I knew she was a trusted source who would listen and offer understanding in an unbiased way, free from judgment. She saw some of the family *hate* I received on social media and offered guidance from both perspectives that really led me to tighten up my boundaries and get clear on what I was willing to tolerate in my personal online spaces. Feeling like I was being cracked open once again, it was just another layer to recognize and heal. The outcome was beautiful … unbeknownst to me it was the pathway that led into my discovery and love of somatics and nervous-system health, and my Rooted In Fear Four-Step somatic tool, course, and supportive card deck.

This was the second year in a row where I noticed that the more I healed and discovered more about myself, the more I created and offered others because of it. It allowed me to shift my thinking from doomsday when I was on the brink of healing something deep, to something more empowering and what I was going to release and receive in the midst of it all. This was certainly a much healthier way to view it, anyways. This experience catapulted me right into my next purpose in life. And this, this lit me up!

I know this topic can raise such deeply personal, charged, and strong beliefs. We are passionate beings who want to be heard and understood, so I love that in you. Remember, it is the very passion within us that helps to advance the world we live in. With so many options out there, religion–New Age, God, spirituality–I would ask you, Reader, to move from a place of love and curiosity if any of this chapter resonates or triggers you. To take moments offering education in a non-threatening or aggressive way, to listen to understand rather than judge. Many of us are searching to find answers, to find ourselves.

And sometimes all we need is a gentle hand, soft voice, and genuine friendship. So, Reader, keep being the open-minded, supportive being you are; the world needs you.

PERMISSION GRANTED to evolve your perspectives and embrace a clearer, more authentic understanding of yourself.

The Breaking Point Era

"Just underneath your breaking point lies your true
strength."

—Jennifer Tindugan-Adoviso

It wasn't just my spirituality, beliefs, and inner conflicts that were in shambles—my family life was taking hits in all directions, too. A tornado is how I can sum up our three years at this duty station.

Every day felt like Groundhog Day. As I woke up, setting my intentions and listing at least three things I was grateful for, I tried to quiet the voice telling me today would be no different than yesterday. I would head into the bathroom with full intentions to remain positive. Showering—check, animals—check, kids—check. I would head off to work in deep thought. Often those drives to and from work offered me the most solace I would have in the day. Work was work. I would leave right on time and walk to the car in anticipation of what I would walk into at home. I braced myself constantly. I don't know normal, so it is hard to say if this is the average person's experience; I just know it was mine.

Getting home, it was like job number two commenced. Many times I was immersed upstairs in my office learning, studying, practicing, and coaching, while Keith was downstairs watching television or scrolling on his phone.

The boys were outside with friends or as immersed in playing video games as I was in studying. What always seemed present, regardless, were the battles, arguments, questions, chaos, alcohol, laziness, walking on eggshells—every bit of that was always there. I remember having a personal coaching session because I felt at my wit's end; I always needed to play referee between my husband and kids. All the stories of the events unfolding didn't seem to match. And the kids' reactions would be alarming, so I didn't have comfort in what to believe. *Certainly my husband wasn't gaslighting the kids, denying them of their reality? They must be exaggerating.* This must have felt disempowering to Keith, but something felt off in my system. Something felt inauthentic not only by his reaction, but theirs, too. I had to trust it.

I recall Jen telling me what she visualized was a tornado and I was getting swooped up instead of taking shelter. *Nope,* I thought to myself. *That isn't going to work for me. Take shelter in the midst of chaos? Chaos is where I thrive. Chaos is where I do best. Chaos is where I have control.* Makes sense, right? That is all my childhood was. Military life breeds the same. My house was just an extension of all of it. Taking shelter didn't feel right or safe. I was a mother to a house full of beautiful and special children who all marched to the beat of their own drum—during this duty station alone we received medical diagnoses of autism, OCD, ADD, ADHD, depression, anxiety and C-PTSD. All gifted in their own unique way, they also triggered the hell out of one another, leaving me feeling on guard. Now add my unhealed inner child into the mix and a spouse who is set in his ways, unwilling to be open-minded to others' point of view—are you seeing the storm within?

My mentor shared with me that I was acting as the referee when I needed to allow things to unfold and be there to repair as needed. Again, that did not feel safe at all. I struggled with this because I saw things I remembered in my childhood: the way Keith spoke to the kids, the way my kids questioned—not to question authority, but rather to question to understand. Keith was often triggered by that and instead of asking follow-up questions, sharing in their curiosity, or offering an educational moment, he would shut them down. We all joked how he should trademark and coin the word *no*, as it seemed to be all he said. It was like that was easiest in those moments for him than to actually think something through. This placed me in protective momma mode because I could see it all happen.

There was so much friction. The drinking was out of hand... for both of us. I questioned him many times, "Are we drinking too much? This just seems like too much?" I gaslit myself a lot. Being raised in a home—two homes, actually—where my parents had substance abuse and dependency issues, I never knew what *normal* was... but then again, what really is *normal?* Crying myself to sleep many nights in confusion, battling the internal chaos, I wondered how we got here.

Because of my work and duty shifts I couldn't drink every single night. The position Keith was in made him exempt from those duties. Logically I knew it was too much; when I heard other people's stories of alcohol dependency and abuse I would realize how parts of their stories very much aligned with mine, with ours. And so again and again I would ask Keith the same questions, and again and again he would snicker at me in disbelief. I should have listened to myself, my body, my intuition. Our nights got later and later, his patience thinner and thinner, our connection further and further apart. I had a spouse who didn't look at me, didn't touch me, didn't compliment me, didn't date me. His number one desire was no longer me—it was alcohol.

Active in my coaching academy, we had to be our own client first. With mentorship oversight, we were taken through various coaching models—Boundaries, Worthy, Relationship Blueprint, Reinvention, amongst others. I had such profound awareness in my discoveries. Each and every time we did reflections it always came back to the same thing... me reflecting on my weight, my alcohol consumption, my nutrition, and my relationship with Keith. And to note... the nutrition, weight, and alcohol all went hand in hand. As far as Keith, I held onto the potential of what could be. I held onto the vision that we could get it back to how it used to be. I held onto knowing who he could be if he would just work on himself as I had been. I stuck it out, also feeling I owed it to him due to my violation of trust at the beginning of our relationship. The love coupled with my deep desire to help people... it seemed only logical in my mind to stay the course.

Through my healing there were just so many "ah-ha's" I had never considered. To put it into a visual, it was like all the ah-ha's were pouring into a funnel but processing them all was too much; the funnel was filling quicker than it could empty. One I struggled to process was feeling like I was being judged all the time. Growing up constantly ridiculed and criticized, I worked in overdrive to try to be perfect, which in part led to so much self-judgment. In this discovery I noticed just how much I also judged. In what I felt was a loving attempt to support Keith and help him realize the ramifications of his thoughts, actions, and behaviors, there was also a subtle judgment for his behavior and the effect it had on everyone in the house.

I also assumed others were judging me, because I was judging myself. I learned at a very young age to constantly evaluate myself and my surroundings because I knew the consequences if I left a mess behind, if I missed a spot on the table or dishes, if my clothes didn't fit right. The attempt to evaluate quickly turned to self-judgment. I highly doubt I crossed the minds of all the people over the years I thought were judging me... talk about self-obsessed! We all are, though, aren't we? How many times do we think other people are thinking things merely because we think it about ourselves? A mentor of mine, Victoria, actually taught me that the shadow of those examples is merely self-obsession. I've had many clients share similar stories. Feeling awkward walking into a room, feeling like all eyes are on them when in reality everybody's just doing their own thing. When I learned of this I was blown away by how someone with such little self-confidence, who was low-maintenance and always put everyone before themselves, could be self-obsessed.

Nothing changed between Keith and I. He remained closed off, uninterested, inactive, and uninvolved. I continued thinking it was me, so I dove more and more into working to "fix" myself. I told myself if I fixed all the things that were wrong with me maybe he would want to take me on a date. Maybe he would hold my hand in the parking lot as we walked into the store together. Hell, maybe he would walk next to me instead of ten paces ahead of me. I continued forcing and pushing, trying to get the opposite from him. But we were both in utter denial. The kids were not happy, I was not happy; we walked and lived on eggshells. This type of living was all too familiar; it was my childhood.

Preparing for my retirement, it was now late spring. I had family and friends from all over coming into town to celebrate and support me in this achievement. It can always be chaotic and crazy when you get people from different walks of life all in one location, but I tried to focus on the purpose and also be in full gratitude that people were willing to come celebrate with me. It was such a fulfilling weekend reminiscing, being with family all under the same roof, playing games, laughing. We went to restaurants on the water, played card games around the dining room table; we even talked about Paris, since Keith and I would be going as my retirement gift and Keith graduation's gift from his master's program. We were in good company.

It was time for my family to start their journeys back home—hugs, "see ya laters," and "thanks for comings" were thrown around the dining room as people shifted to the door to leave. There were a few family members and my girlfriend who stayed a little bit longer. We decided to spend the day outside, grab lunch, move, do some shopping, and have cocktails, of course; everything always involved cocktails. We went to a cute, quaint town; it was a favorite and had everything right there. I walked off with my mom and my friend, heading into a little shop while Keith walked off into another store to look for some new clothes. Time passed by, and we were ready to head back. All giddy and happy about the occasion, the sun actually out instead of the usual gloom we typically have, I walked down the sidewalk and found the store Keith was in to let him know we were done. Walking up to the store I could see through the glass window. He was laughing, smiling, and carrying on with the two women at the cash register. My heart sank. I felt a pit in my stomach. Blocking the tears from swelling in my eyes, I thought to myself, *I haven't seen his face this lit up in years. I can't remember the last time he looked at me and laughed like that.* Wanting to vomit, feeling trembling in my legs, I immediately sensed, *I've been here before. I know what this means.*

Dismissing my feelings, I thought, *Candice, stop. This is no big deal—why are you upset? You are being dramatic and overreacting. Enough!* Those were the words I told myself as I took a deep breath and got it together. I knew it was pointless to have a conversation about this. Not only had he been drinking, he just wasn't going to see it the way I did. We met back up with everyone else, got in the car, and headed home. Later that night I had to take the rest of the crew back to the airport. I remember sobbing on the way home. Feeling so alone in our relationship, I started questioning, *Am I too fat? Is it my gray hair, my wrinkles? I'm not in my twenties or thirties anymore—am I just not aging gracefully?* Tears continued streaming down my face as I looked out the car window in contemplation. Feelings of unworthiness ripped through my entire body, and then I was suddenly reminded, *I will always find evidence to support my beliefs.* Unfortunately, I had a garden full of weeds... weeds that kept growing because I'd watered them over and over through the years. I didn't have the awareness to know I needed to pull them out at the root. So, season through season, I have focused on finding all the evidence to prove my beliefs to be true, this instance being another.

Now on terminal leave from the military—paid time used to transition from military to civilian life—I was learning and discovering my new normal. What did my days look like without reporting to someone? What did my days look like without deadlines? What did my days look like without having to work out? Without having to go through extreme dieting to meet the military's body composition requirements twice a year? To not have overnight duties, missing days with my family? To not be on edge waiting to be told I'm going to deploy? What did all this look like? Talk about a new beginning.

The terminal leave went by quickly, and it was such an odd process. Here I thought detaching from the military would be this big celebration and I would transition effortlessly, creating my new normal while running my business. That I would have all this time to manage the household for balance and feel that inner peace I had craved for so long.

In my mind this entire transition was supposed to be exciting. Instead, I was met with so many appointments. I didn't realize how much my body had been compensating for me, and now that it was able to take a giant deep breath, I felt it all. I had weekly EMDR trauma therapy sessions, physical therapy for my pelvic organ prolapse twice per week, physical therapy for my frozen shoulder twice per week, and weekly dry-needling sessions to help release the muscle tension living in my shoulder. Everything about me shifted. No energy, my spark was gone—there were days I didn't shower and brushing my teeth was my greatest achievement. I was packing on weight rapidly. I refused to work out as it triggered old beliefs and patterns of my career's physical expectations of me. I was drinking every day to self-soothe even though I had a desire to quit. Binge eating daily even though I knew I needed to fuel my body better. I was in such bad shape—I had to hold onto the banister just to walk down the stairs. I was urinating on myself. I couldn't use my right arm. I remember thinking to myself, *No wonder my husband wants nothing to do with me. What have I become?*

We had our Paris trip in just a couple weeks so we ventured out shopping for something nice to wear since we would be visiting a Michelin-star restaurant. We both struggled to find something to wear. We were larger than we desired. We were so used to uniforms and sweats, we didn't even know where to begin. I thought if we just quit drinking we wouldn't eat as much and we wouldn't be as heavy as we were. But every time I would mention it, Keith invalidated and dismissed those thoughts.

We were really excited for this trip; it had been years since he and I had been together on a trip fully immersed in one another. I was really looking forward to this! We needed this. I remember loading the plane and off we went to Paris, France. I had these expectations of reconnecting and reigniting the spark between us that seemed to have fizzled out. Seems appropriate being in Paris, right? What I learned early on in my healing is that expectations lead to disappointment. You see, I had these expectations that we were going to be hand in hand frolicking down the streets of Paris. I envisioned affection, attention, intimacy—the version of Keith and Candice that sits in the forefront of my mind and memories. The Keith and Candice that is there somewhere very deep, covered in life's to-do lists, kids, work. But it was like we never left home.

The night of our Michelin-star dinner, I was so excited to get dolled up. Staring into the mirror I curled sections of my hair, spraying hair spray and alternating the heat to keep the curl. As my hair set, I moved onto my face; I used all my favorite products. Last, the fake lashes and the matte lipstick and gloss to seal the look. One final look in the mirror, and I felt pretty. I felt like it had been a long time since I'd seen this version of Candice. Not thrilled with the extra chin that seemed to still stand out, I focused on my eyes and their twinkle that seemed to come alive. I noticed my ear-to-ear smile that was real, and my light.

Ready to reveal myself, ready for a romantic date with my husband in PARIS, I opened the double sliding door to step out of the bathroom where he stood looking at himself in the mirror. He turned toward me and said... "You all ready?" My breath felt as if it had left my body. I paused for a moment then replied with, "Yes." That was it. That was my moment. We headed down to the hotel lobby where we waited for our Uber ride. Standing outside in the chilly evening, still trying to find my breath, I waited for him to tell me I looked nice. Something, anything that offered me validation that I still had it. That we still had it. We got into the car and I quietly sat, staring out the window and thinking to myself, *How am I in Paris and I can't even get a compliment all dressed up?* Trying not to mess up my makeup, I felt my eyes swelling. *This is going to be messy,* I thought, holding back tears. Avoiding eye contact with him, the build-up crowded my eyes and then released. One by one the tears fell, streaming down my face. He couldn't see me. Holding in the bellows that wanted to release, I tucked them somewhere within so I didn't ruin the night.

We arrived at the restaurant and had a few minutes to wait before they opened. He could tell something was wrong with me. "Are you alright?" he asked. Sharing with him my disappointment and hurt feelings, he stood there and stared at me, speechless, followed by, "I told you in the fitting room at the store that you looked nice in this dress." Shutting down, feeling unattractive and disconnected, I put on my mask, smiling the rest of the evening.

Was I expecting too much, am I too much, am I too needy? My head filled with all of it. *I am not pretty enough, I am not skinny enough, I am not good enough. It's the weight,* I contemplated.

Our Paris trip wound to a close without the relationship restoration I'd hoped for. When we returned home, Keith and I had deep discussions about what went wrong on our trip. I spent the next few therapy sessions worried it was all my fault. That I'd ruined Paris because I was too needy and had too high of expectations. *Great—more layers for me to peel back,* I told myself. *More brokenness within me I have to heal. I am the problem in this relationship. I am projecting all my trauma onto him,* I told myself… and him. *It is my fault the relationship has shifted. He is such a good man to tolerate me. I am so lucky he stands by me through all of this.* I shared with him that this was a *me* problem and I would get better. That these situations were just highlighting what I needed to heal within.

As the days went on, the more withdrawn I got, the more weight I gained, the more I was numb and disassociated. *Is this what major depression feels like? I thought.* I was still trying to work my business, create programs and content, and take on one-on-one clients. It was amazing how I could see so clearly for others but felt so blind trying to navigate and help myself.

In May, the week of Mother's Day, I was given a retreat by a beautiful friend. I got to attend Deepak Chopra's wellness retreat in Arizona. That week I was gone brought me a heightened awareness of myself. This is where I was fully introduced to somatics. During yoga, I was doing a pose and suddenly my right leg started shaking uncontrollably. At first I thought I'd overstretched. And then the yoga instructor came over to me, gently placed her hand on my back, and said, "Allow it." She educated me that I was having a somatic release. We had done so much hip work and stretching, twice a day while being there, I was having a massive physical and energetic release. Out of nowhere I was bawling. Like hard-core bawling. In my head like I often am, I was trying to figure out what I was letting go of. Then I realized it didn't matter. It was no longer trapped in my body. I remember crying so hard while also feeling embarrassed. I was strong. And strong isn't breaking down in a room full of women you don't know. But once I allowed the release in my fullest expression, others followed. The room became an expression of pain. Pain that, you could tell by the bellows, had been waiting years to be released. It was beautiful and sad all in the same breath; it's the duality in life we get the pleasure of witnessing. When we were done, this incredibly beautiful woman came over to me and said, "I am so glad that I heard you cry. Your crying allowed me to cry." I told her, "I am so happy to have been your permission slip." She smiled and nodded. "Yes, that's exactly what you were, my permission slip.".

Journal Entry

Today was tough. I met resistance during our yoga as I connected with the movement of my hips. Such tightness, such soreness — it really mirrored the emotional state I was in. As I moved through this connection honoring my intention, the yoga instructor lightly touched me; it was like the Universe was reminding me of my promise to self. I felt safe; I felt as though it was time to let it go. What, I did not know. I suddenly realized, "But I don't want to." It was not the release I didn't want to experience or feel, but rather what the release represented. Letting go of you, Dad, little by little takes away our connection. I would rather feel pain than not feel any of you.

I headed home feeling refreshed, rejuvenated, and educated. I had learned some invaluable things at the retreat, and everyone I met left a lasting impression on me. Funny how that is… all of us strangers brought together *by chance* and leaving having impacting one another. That's pure divine intervention. I remember getting home, and it was full speed ahead. We sold our home and would be closing to move mid-June. I spent the coming weeks purging closets and throwing away old picture albums and nursing material that no longer needed to occupy physical space. I put aside all my military manuals, uniforms, and other items that didn't need to come along. As I was purging the spaces in my home, I was also purging spaces within. Coming across pictures of lil' Candice, petty officer Candice, and officer Candice, it was like all versions of me hit at once. I remember telling Keith I needed to pause for a moment. Finding my bootcamp photo and commissioning photo and knowing the timeline and events between them made me so emotional. I remember thinking, *If lil' Candice only knew what she would be facing in the coming years.* Putting the lil' Candice picture down and picking up the bootcamp photo, I thought, *If this version of her only knew what was coming her way. The fights she would have to armor up for. The hits, physically, she would be taking.* I was so emotional in the living room as I shared all this with Keith. Finally, I picked up the commissioning photo and said, "I did it. I did what they all said I couldn't, and more. But man, she's tired, weighed down and broken. She's suffocating and can't breathe."

I felt so much love and compassion for myself as I viewed the photos, uniforms, and books and reminisced about old relationships. I couldn't believe how much time had gone by and how much I had held onto, both literally and figuratively. There was such an emotional connection to many of the items. Keith, on the other hand, was ecstatic because we kept dragging the stuff with us each time we moved. Each time we purged, he gently mentioned those bins and boxes, and I would always find a reason why I needed to keep them. But this time was different. I am not sure if it was all the internal releases at the retreat that canceled out some of the stuff I was holding onto, but nonetheless, it was time to let it all go.

Speaking of the great purge, Keith and I didn't *fight,* because Keith didn't purge any emotions or feelings. I would share my annoyance with him or discuss how I didn't like something he said, but for the most part I was not one to internalize and let things fester. I knew that wasn't healthy in a relationship and I welcomed conflict because I felt like we could talk things out in a healthy way. On the other hand, he internalized every single thing. If I were to fart on him walking by and it bothered him, he would not say a word and just roll his eyes and let it go. If I came across as too assertive in a discussion, he wouldn't say anything. Many years. Many annoyances. Many irritations.

Many frustrations. Him not saying anything after years reared its head, and next thing I knew it was the end of May and we were in a deep discussion about his unhappiness. The words he shared—"The grass might be greener on the other side"—made me realize I had been his only serious relationship. He wasn't sure. He knew he was fearful to be alone and didn't know what decision to make. It was like a grenade to the face. Just back from a retreat, sold our home, purged all our stuff, and out of nowhere, *I don't know if I want to be together anymore.*

I was gutted. *How did this happen? How is he saying this to me? What have I done wrong?* I asked him so many questions as I sat on my bed in our bedroom staring out to the greenbelt. Numb. In shock. Feeling not enough, inadequate, too this, too that. The stories of "they all leave me" flooded my entire internal cavity. I remained upstairs to avoid attention and alerting the kids. I cried. I sobbed. In an emotional spiral and denial, I wondered in curiosity how I hadn't seen this. I wondered how I'd overlooked it all. I even wondered how he was considering the grass on the other side when we were the ones dealing with all his toxicity shaming, belittling, walking on eggshells.

Handling the situation like I had for so many others in my life, I stepped out. I drove to a parking lot and cried. I called my friend Brooke, my spiritual teacher and mentor, to speak openly and honestly about what was going on. Her wisdom of reminding me to connect to myself, to ground was what I needed and welcomed. I needed to give myself permission to disconnect from the chaos the world was presenting me, not by avoiding it, but by connecting to the wisdom within to feel into what it was *I* wanted and needed. I knew I wanted to be with him. He was my spouse.

We had been through so much together. *I am not giving up now,* I thought to myself.

After a couple hours sitting in the car chatting with Brooke and another friend, listening to music, grounded, connecting, I decided to head back to the house. Sitting on the couch, still numb, I stared out at the greenbelt. It was my therapy. The trees, the animals, the sunset—it all felt so peaceful, which was what I needed in that now moment. As Keith sat on the couch adjacent to me, crying, which was a first, he just stared off into the opposite direction of the room with an occasional glance in my direction. Keith didn't show much emotion. It was something I struggled for years to understand, until I did. I asked him why he was crying, to which he replied, "I feel like I failed. I have been a coward so wrapped up in work, bad habits, and even perfecting my golf game instead of trying to work on our marriage." He was open and shared some things that upset him during our time at that duty station, some things that blew my mind and could have been immediately adjusted had I known. My heart sank; I was sad with a splash of anger at why he wouldn't have shared these things with me over the years.

I remember sitting on the couch, still staring out the window and saying a prayer to myself, asking for a sign that it was going to be better. That we would figure out a way through this. I got up and headed to the kitchen to make something to eat since I had not eaten all day. As I went to the microwave to grab my food, he stopped me and wrapped his six-foot arms around me, asking me to forgive him and give him a chance to do better. The relief I felt that he wanted to make this work, that he loved and valued our relationship to at least give it a try made me so happy. There was also hesitancy and nervousness in my physical body to uproot all my kids to the other coast, leaving my daughter, and close on this new construction home if in fact it didn't work. But I couldn't allow fear to sit in the driver's seat. I had to trust what he said: his personal therapy, marriage counseling, and better work/life balance would support us in making the changes necessary.

Every time we moved he would always say, "Next duty station will be better" and then list off a long list of why the current one was awful. And like clockwork, he said it. This time, though, having seen his pattern, I couldn't sit and listen to it. I was also seeing things so differently and just couldn't enable the thought by nodding in agreement. Simply put, I didn't agree. Maybe insensitive of me, but I had shifted and grown so much I knew enough that the way we view things is merely a reflection of our own inner world. Offering compassion and also tough love that a wife in honesty would share, I said, "Keith, you are the common denominator in all your duty stations, relationships, and experiences. Maybe it's your outlook that needs to pivot. Why have all these places been terrible?" He swore this new duty station would be better and rattled off a list of whys. "Keith, I hear all of that but the location isn't going to change your habits, it isn't going to change you wanting to leave the house, it isn't going to change how you treat everyone." Welcoming my feedback, he still felt it would be different. I had to trust him to follow through, to take radical responsibility. To be honest, it felt good getting all his feelings out and into the open.

I had so many opportunities in this era for me to look and listen to the wisdom within. This era left me so internally conflicted. Sometimes I knew my trauma and projections were driving my thoughts, actions, and behavior, others, I gaslit myself and my own personal knowing. I was so rooted in being accepted and loved, and had been told or made to feel so much over the years; I was the problem—why would these situations be any different? Me, an anxious attachment style constantly seeking external validation and reassurance, likely overwhelmed Keith's system. And Keith, with an avoidant attachment style, handling inner and outer conflicts by shutting down, activated and overwhelmed my system. While nothing was wrong with either of us, these differences created a wedge, a ripple in our communication, and overall in our marriage. Reader, if you felt connected to any piece of this era, I ask you to be gentle with yourself. Start slowly by connecting with yourself and listening, truly listening, to your body's wisdom. This sacred vessel is always in support of you. Sometimes our life gives us the illusion of what we want to see, but in the connection to self, you know.

PERMISSION GRANTED to honor your intuition and set boundaries that support your well-being.

The Recalibration Era

"When we surrender, the chaos becomes our
connection."

—Candice West

The boys and I arrived at the next destination! Keith
would be joining us in a couple weeks but because of
our closing date and the animals' transportation, we headed
out earlier. By this time I'd had zero break from the boys—
long days in the car cross-country, one hotel room to share
to cut down on expenses, and a whole summer to go. I
remember feeling so incredibly blessed, though. Blessed to
be retired and have the flexibility I did. Blessed to have the
financial capacity. Blessed to have this time with them.

We closed on the house and were in! July 1 and our
household goods were delivered. It felt like Christmas in
July! The movers spent the day unloading all our
belongings while I tried to navigate and direct traffic,
ensuring all the boxes and furniture ended up in the correct
rooms. We were all so exhausted by the end of the day none
of us had any desire to start unboxing a thing. The boys and
I voted—plopping onto the couch we decided to binge
watch *The Mole* on Netflix until we couldn't keep our eyes
open any longer. This was also the day Keith got on the road
and started his trek home to us.

The next day I dug right in. With no rhyme or rhythm, the three of us focused on one box at a time. I knew the kitchen needed to get done so I could start preparing meals at home. Not only was I tired of restaurants, but it was so expensive. I had just gotten off the phone with Keith and he was checking into his hotel for night two. He'd traveled so many miles already, he was going to be able to arrive the next day, which blew my mind since it had taken me three-and-a-half days. But then again, he didn't have the boys, who needed to stop what felt like every couple hours. We hung up, and I went back to it. Hours passed and I was still in the kitchen. I kept asking myself how on earth we had accumulated so much, and then I realized it was because Keith always found fun gadgets to give me, hoping it would make something easier on me. And maybe because I couldn't seem to throw any of them away even after fourteen years.

I was finally down to the last few boxes in the kitchen, but it looked like an absolute disaster. Keith called, asking if I needed anything from Target. I was so confused. That's when he said he would be home soon. After checking into his hotel earlier in the evening, he decided to make the rest of the trip since he felt fine and the weather was good. So now, in just an hour, my husband would be with us at our new house. Another new beginning with work-life balance, my dedicated business schedule, lots of space, so many things to do for family fun, and an opportunity to rebuild our marriage. It felt good. It felt peaceful. It felt aligned.

Keith arrived a little later that evening and I was so happy to see him. I greeted him with a big hug—I'd missed him. He was greeted by the boys and the animals and received a tour of the new house. Still wired from the long drive, we did what we seemed to do best lately—cocktails, TV, and bed, in that order.

We spent the following couple of days unpacking and trying to get organized. My phone rang, and it was my mom. It was just after July 4, and she was informing me that something happened between her and her husband. Over the course of the next week she managed to relapse on cocaine and get arrested for domestic violence. She spent the following weeks calling me all hours of the day and night, distraught, heartbroken, and lost. It was so hard to feel bad for her since the details she shared with me revealed her current state was self-inflicted. Her sharing this information with me felt gross. It felt like I was complicit. I wanted nothing to do with any of it as I was trying to focus on my family and all we were navigating. And also, I felt like I was abandoning her by not taking the phone calls and listening to her ramble on under the influence. My inner conflict was screaming. The codependency was hollering. My abandoned, alone, discarded inner child was in pain.

Keith would hear her through the phone just going on and on, not understanding why I didn't just hang up. Heck, I couldn't understand myself, I suppose. Those were the moments I felt so much jealousy for my husband. How he could just detach from emotions and follow the logic. I didn't want to feel pain; I also didn't want to feel responsible for someone else's. I tried to put myself in her shoes and knew I would want support from family. I understood her unaddressed trauma. And while I had compassion for that, it got to a point where it was becoming unhealthy for me.

One day, I found myself swimming in the awareness of the shoe story back at fifteen years old. After learning my mom was on drugs back then, I was enraged. Suddenly, I was on fire, activated, throat burning, heart racing... doing *the work*, I let it rip. I screamed so loudly I frightened my poor dogs: "Mom, you're such an asshole! You were willing to let me go, to kick me out over what would equate to a night of getting high with your boyfriend." This watered all the seeds. The entire garden. The thoughts cycled over and over through my head, *The drugs were more important than me. The abusive man was more important than me.* I was flooded with memory after memory of all I had been through—her drug use, witnessing violent domestic altercations with her partner, and the various levels of abuse and neglect my siblings and I had endured as children.

Knowing her responses were rooted in her own personal trauma, there was pity for her but there was also aggravation. By her not doing *the work*, my siblings and I had endured so much more. I worried about my mom, I loved her, but I knew it was not healthy for me to be involved like this.

With my job as a nurse and life coach, I felt deep guilt and inner conflict for having such strong feelings toward her behavior. But I couldn't give her excuses. I was not going to be codependent. We all have a responsibility to seek help when we recognize we have a problem, and though she recognized it, knew it, even, she refused—what was missing was the desire to get better. She wasn't ready. I was at a crossroads where I had to choose. *Do I continue expending my energy, time, and tears on someone who just doesn't get it and needs to hit rock bottom, or do I let go and choose me? Focus on my family that needs me?* The decision felt very clear to me one night after a conversation where she, again, was under the influence of something and breaking the law. I wanted no part in it. After deep reflection and conversation with Keith, I made a decision. Until further notice, it was a no-contact relationship, with sincere prayers she got the help and support she needed.

Journal Entry

I can't enable her.

I have a part in this, and that is to do it differently than I ever have.

Love her from a distance. I can't save her.

I have to release during this time feeling responsible and obligated to help and fix her situations.

I need to switch that energy and place it into myself.

Self-care is not selfish!

Aside from all my mom's shenanigans, we were also living our own lives trying to get settled in our new home. This move was so unique in that I would not be reporting for duty. This was our first time moving together where I wasn't checking in or attending a college or training program. It helped reduce the pressure and stress of needing to unpack quickly; we welcomed that change. We spent the coming weeks and months not only unpacking but creating spaces that felt comfortable and like home. We got creative with color, DIY accent walls, and even dimensional contact paper in my office, which was a favorite. It felt nice not to rush. Not to have bare walls. To be creative and explore all the different possibilities.

As the days and months went along I noticed I no longer had the desire to drink. I found myself cutting back drastically; my food consumption even started shifting. I was becoming more intentional and listening to myself when it came to intuitive nudges to try new things, detaching from expectations, fears, and outcomes. Which actually led me to my new love—pilates. I remember seeing the advertisement on social media and thought, *OMG, this looks like fun.* I debated going because of the stories I told myself about the kind of girls who do pilates and yoga—the skinny, flexible girls. I made a decision and went anyway, forcing myself to trust my wisdom within. I could not have been more wrong. Women of all colors, shapes, sizes, and ages were there. I felt so at home I signed up for an unlimited package and built a beautiful relationship with this new form of movement. I was attending at least four times a week, had friends for the first time in what felt like forever, and my business was starting to build traction, which I was thrilled about given that I had just relocated.

Being open to new possibilities and the wisdom within, I even gave myself permission to explore mentors and make big decisions listening solely to my body's sensations. Things just seemed to be improving. What was not improving was the relationship between Keith and I. He had even later nights, always with drinking involved. He was grumpy and short-fused and I was walking on eggshells, feeling disgusted at how he was not keeping his word on seeking support for himself and us as a couple. But I knew I could not be the driver in this. I had to sit and let him take action. If this was something he really wanted, he would follow through on his promise to me, to us. I had to be in the energy of full surrender, no matter how hard it was for me. And it was hard. I had been the one in the driver's seat of our relationship for the last several years, and I knew I was not going to force it. I had to remain focused on me, healing me, and doing what I could do to better me. *No action is action.*

Late fall and my sister Jennifer and her littles came to visit. We were all excited to see them. Heck, even meet them! I had not met the littlest addition yet as he was born while we were stationed on the west coast. We thoroughly enjoyed the company, getting outside the house and going to the park, lunch, and even the trampoline park. It was so nice to witness everyone playing like little kids, even the adults. I also noticed a break in walking on eggshells and hearing the condescending and belittling comments from Keith over the weekend. That alerted me and had me in deep thought about *why. Why was it so easy to be nice when we had visitors and why could he not have this kind of self-control everyday?* I thought.

Once we caught our breath from the busy weekend, I remember noticing the shift in Keith almost immediately. I couldn't help but ask how it was that he was so kind, friendly, and enjoyable to be around all weekend but now he was a different person. The person we were all familiar with. "I was in 'hosting' mode," he shared. I remember thinking, *How on earth can one just shift personas like that?* And then quickly I recalled, *Me, that's who.* I immediately realized I was so triggered by it because that had been me for years. And, in some ways, it still was. I just let that sit with me. I also noticed the judgment I had toward him for being "fake" when in reality it must have been extremely challenging for him, with his sensory overload, to have my sister and all her small kids in the home on top of our two children and the four animals. I quickly reframed my thinking, my attitude, and met him with compassion, asking what support he needed: to nap, play video games, or even hit golf balls on the simulator in the garage.

This served as an important reminder to myself that even though I have healed in many ways and have a better awareness and understanding, it doesn't mean others are in the same place. It also revealed to me I still live in judgment. Once I caught myself and looked at him with grace, the disgust was replaced with compassion. And this, my friends, is an example of why doing *the work* is not only healing for you but also those around you.

I credit this quick pivot to the intense somatic practitioner program I had started earlier in the fall. I was learning a lot of new and amazing things that were allowing me to recognize and track my triggers at a deeper level. This offered me so much insight into me. It is not usually about the other person when we can lay our ego to rest. When we can get to a healthy place to realize that and see what the situation is offering us, we can develop a deeper self connection and course correct where and when needed. Some situations just are what they are, but I believe there is always something we can learn in these situations when we give ourselves permission to take a step back.

The holidays were here, and we had a full house. Starting off with Thanksgiving, Nattie and her boyfriend flew in from Washington State, and my brother-in-law, his girlfriend, and the in-laws drove up from Florida. This was such a different dynamic for me because it was the first time during any of the holidays we'd all spent together where I chose to not drink. It came as a shock when I would turn it down. Heck, I shocked myself. For me, it definitely felt different. I was used to sipping on wine while baking desserts for Thanksgiving Day, and here I had a Stanley water bottle. I didn't mind everyone else drinking, but it definitely allowed me to see things differently than before.

Thanksgiving morning, mimosas were being passed around and again, no desire. A crooked look from Keith with a mumble of "okay" as he passed mine on to someone else. At that moment I felt fear. I felt my desire to no longer drink was going to create another crack in our foundation. It was something we always did together. Football—cocktails. Movies—cocktails. Stressed—cocktails. Celebration—cocktails. It was always there, hiding discreetly off in the background, but really what drove our connection and disconnection. We spent the day watching football, everyone making commentary on each play while predicting who was going to win. Eating all the yummy food prepared that day and the evening before, laughter filled the house; we are all such unique characters. And of course, it wouldn't be a family affair without the in-laws going back and forth while making their appetizers. And then winding down the night watching random movies as a family of one. That night, I had a glass of wine in the evening and again found myself not interested in drinking it. I had a few sips and even those felt forced. I thought to myself, *What is going on with me?* I knew deep down it wasn't a bad thing and was a true answer to many evening prayers, but I was also curious how one day there was just zero desire to consume alcohol after it had been a staple in my life and my way to *feel better*.

Next up was Florida, Universal Studios. We decided to really focus on experiences for the kids since they were all older and understood all the truths about Santa Claus. We were tired of wasting money on video games and other things that ended up in the corner of closets so we decided on a last-minute family trip. We were pretty excited to go! We kept the location from the boys so they would have some excitement when we left. They didn't know what state we were going to until we got to the airport; the suspense was killing them.

Once we arrived, they were so stoked. I could see their faces light up; Keith's inner child was coming out, which made me so happy to witness. He was always so on edge and high strung at home so to see him chill, laughing and smiling, sober, was a breath of fresh air.

I remember one night while we were still at the park and waiting for a ride to reopen that was shut down, watching the castle light show. There is something about the music that gets me every single time. It is a nostalgic feeling that brews within listening to the music while watching the lights and the creativity of it all. I thought to myself, *Wow, I am here. I am happy. I am with my family. It has been a minute since I have felt this kind of joy. Not rushing, just flowing. No alcohol, just water. Funnel cakes and pretzels. My kids and my adult kid are just looking so happy and having the time of their life. This! This is what I want to feel every day. But why not? What is so different here than at home?* I pondered that question while I watched the light show, feeling a few subtle tears roll down my cheek. *Why does it take vacations to soak in togetherness? Why does it take special occasions to book the vacation? Why isn't togetherness found at home where we are together daily?* So much went through my mind, and I decided I was going to make some personal changes that would allow me to share in my family's togetherness a little more authentically and intentionally when I got back home.

Self-connection goes beyond the hobbies, the pedicures, the pilates class. It is an understanding that all you desire is hidden deep within your soul, ready to be accessed and awakened. When you start calling out to your desires, when you whisper your needs, when you demand more, when you hope and pray for better or different, don't be surprised when it all flows right to you when you are not expecting it. This recalibration was what I needed to reunite to self. To trust self. To welcome all of self. If you see yourself in this chapter, Reader, know that the invitations look subtle, and sometimes they slap you across the face, knocking all the air from your lungs. But I called it all in. I asked for change. I asked for healing. I asked for my wholeness and truth to be revealed to me so I could come home to self. Don't be fearful of what is in store. Don't allow the resistance to keep you in the same cycles, swimming the same drains, when you are deeply craving more. You've got this, one day, one moment at a time.

PERMISSION GRANTED to embrace clarity and fulfillment in your daily life.

The Rebuilding Era

"Denial keeps us blind to the things we don't want to
see because our minds don't feel
we're ready to handle them."

—Ken Seeley

Pivoting from my normal holiday routine schedule due
to our holiday trip, I waited to do the majority of all the
baking until we returned. Peanut butter blossoms, Santa
snacks, sugar cookies, snickerdoodles... so many baked
goods I would spend the remainder of the month making
for the family to munch on as we rang in the new year.
Christmas music playing in the background, my favorite
scented candles—I look forward to this time every year.
Keith was back and forth between work and home due to
holiday routine, leave, and special liberty to celebrate the
Christmas and New Year holidays. Our routine was
definitely thrown off but I was enjoying all this time with
the family since my days were usually spent alone at home
tending to the animals, my business, and chores. The kids
typically got home from school and would rush to their
rooms for video games or to the park to play basketball, and
Keith would come home and either drift off napping or was
tied to the TV watching golf, football, or the news. Crazy
how one can have a house so full but feel so alone.

It was late one evening and per usual, TV and cocktails it was, although none for me. I continued to pull back more and more and not really drink after that moment at the Universal Studios light show. I was not interested. We continued watching a series we had been binging and I knew it was getting late… it seemed that's how it went; the nights seemed to be getting later and later as the months passed by. I was getting so tired and knew after this episode I was calling it. Knowing it was wrapping up, I started gathering my things as Keith was getting up. But instead of heading to the sink to dump the ice in his glass, he walked toward our bar station and pulled the cabinet open to make another. "Are you making another drink?" I asked him. "Yeah," he replied. "It is 2 a.m.," I informed him. "But we started another episode," he rebutted. He continued making the drink and came back to the couch, unpausing the TV show. Sitting there in utter and complete shock, I thought to myself, *What just happened? I have lived this life, I know what this means… it literally was my childhood.* I told him I would be going to bed. With a palpable sigh, he drank half the drink as he stood up to conclude the night. I remember walking upstairs telling myself I had to confront him, that I can't and won't live like this.

I wondered if it had always been like this. I questioned how it snuck up on us and got this bad. I questioned how he couldn't see a problem. It made me scared for us. I already felt so alone but knew it was the alcohol that was the wedge between us. I had been trying for so long to have him get help in terms of the childhood issues he kept inside. I touched base on other things throughout the marriage to see what I could do differently. If I was making things harder on him. If my betrayal was in fact an unrepairable crack in the foundation. And each and every time I was told everything was fine. I was fine. He was fine. I had been forgiven, to stop bringing it up. I knew this was his way of coping because it had also been me. I understood it all too well.

The next day I journaled heavily on what it was I needed to say to him. What it was I was feeling. And what I was willing to accept and not accept. I waited in anticipation all day for him to come home, not knowing what his mood or energy would be like. When he finally came home he was so tired. I was met with frustration as I looked over to the couch watching him sleep, knowing I would be handling all the responsibilities of the boys and dinner. I started to feel like his mother. Like a babysitter to a grown man. Irritated and annoyed, I said, "Keith, it has been thirty minutes. You need to wake up or you won't sleep tonight and be in the same position tomorrow." He continued sleeping for two hours while I took over managing the evening duties. I was beyond angry. I was again reminded just how familiar this felt.

Dinner was served and then per usual TV and cocktails, for one. I started doing a lot of thinking about life, its meaning, and even had thoughts pour through, *Is this the kind of life I want to continue living*? It was not enjoyable. It was lonely and, in many ways, toxic. My marriage felt like it was missing several key components, and also, maybe this was normal. Remember, never experiencing healthy relationships before, I always battled myself. I was just now starting to build self-trust. Just starting to listen to the nudges and intuition. I wholeheartedly believed he loved me, but he definitely wasn't showing me in ways that allowed me to feel it. There were parts of me that wondered if I was wasting my time but then I felt smothered in guilt considering leaving the man who had stood by me all these years. Through thick and thin, right?

The following day he came home and spent some time like he usually did unloading his work-day frustrations. I shared that I needed to have a conversation with him. He was open to it. "Keith," I started, "I am really concerned with the drinking. You were pouring another drink at 2 a.m." He immediately became defensive, "It was not two in the morning." Firmly in my truth, I voiced I would not allow myself to be gaslit and manipulated. I continued sharing his cycle that replayed nightly and how I was being left with the responsibilities. I expressed my frustration and sadness in how he would speak to the boys and the feelings of walking on eggshells because we don't know the mood he was in. I let it all out in the most loving, soft way I could. He ended that part of the conversation with, "I had already thought of doing an alcohol-free challenge in the New Year—a ninety-day one." "That is great, I will join you," I shared in relief. I could see on his face that he heard me. I could see he was disappointed in himself. I could see there was something else, but I could not put my finger on it.

We talked about the balance in the home and some other things because I had not seen any efforts to move forward with his promises he had made before leaving the last duty station. No attempts for therapy or marriage counseling. We talked about it all, putting it all out on the table. His response was one I had heard prior, "I will get on it." I felt a bit of emptiness by his response. The fact I was having to remind him of something that had been circling my mind for months, waiting on for months... well, it just made me so sad. I felt like he didn't care. Like he really didn't want to try. Almost like he was just giving up. It didn't help that he avoided communication and confrontation at all costs. I was often left in the dark about where he stood on things, trying to figure it out on my own based on his subtle words, actions, or inactions.

Journal Entry

This year I want more internal peace.

I would love to get my violin repaired and fixed so I can learn to start playing again.

I have many goals this year: lose weight, build my business, in-person retreats, violin, and travel. I see where some of these are already in the works.

I need to find the "it." The "it" that is disconnected with my desires. Perhaps as I continue in the following days and weeks it will become highlighted so I can begin to take intentional action.

The beginning of the new year was rough. Anyone who drinks as many years straight as he did and quits cold turkey is going to be moody, tired, and on edge. I tried to manage everything and support him while also doing my own healing work. Still in both my somatic practitioner programs, I was doing intense work on myself. Purging parents, friends, thoughts, ideas, and beliefs, I was deep in *the work.*

It was a Friday evening and we all decided to go out for dinner. While at the table we chatted about going home afterwards and watching a family movie together. As we left it was pouring, thundering even. During this torrential downpour we all ran laughing toward the car—it gave little kid childhood vibes. Mud puddles splashed with each stride. I was so focused on not slipping I definitely got the most wet out of us all. We headed home and the kids scattered to their rooms while Keith put on some random movie, *Godzilla vs. Kong*. I remember thinking to myself, *He knows darn well I have zero desire to watch this; I hope this is not his idea of a family movie.* "Keith, are we going to watch a movie?" I asked subtly. Pointing to the TV he referenced it was on. "Keith, you know I have zero desire to watch that," I shared, staring at him with a grin. He looked back at me with irritation. And that was it, that was the trigger; I was ready to let it rip. "I feel like I am invisible half the time. Why wouldn't we browse together to pick out something we both want to watch?" I asked. Staring at his phone, he just ignored me. Feeling so invisible, misunderstood, and ignored, I got up and went to the bedroom and decided to read instead. A couple hours later I decided to go to bed; I cried myself to sleep that night, wondering what was happening to us.

The next morning I headed downstairs; Keith was already up. He asked how I slept and how I felt, which were typical questions he asked me daily. I clung to those because it was those questions each day that made me feel like he still cared. Like we were still connected. I sat down on the couch and contemplated mentioning the night prior and how I felt like we needed to talk to clear the air. I battled myself, feeling like sparking the conversation was going to cause problems. I knew he hated these conversations but I also didn't want to compartmentalize it. So, I went for it. In our discussion back and forth we talked about everything… therapy, marriage counseling, balance, his work—you name it, we covered it. One thing that kept sticking out to me were what felt like *excuses* as to why things were the way they were. Something just felt off, again. I couldn't deny my intuition because I had been healed enough to finally gain the confidence to start trusting it. It had been proving to me over the course of months that it was and had been spot on in many moments in my life, both past and present.

That's when I said it. I unloaded it all regardless of how I felt it might be perceived or even make me look. I told him that I am rebuilding a business, working from home during the day after moving to support him, managing all the kids' school stuff and appointments, house chores, groceries, and it felt like his only job was going to work and back. It felt like I was doing everything I could to keep him from burning out since that seemed to be his concern every time I would try to address something. So I kept taking on more and more to lessen his load; meanwhile, I was burning myself out. I told him I felt like that was an excuse. Maybe a poor choice of words at the time. I told him I was constantly trying to encourage him to pour into himself so he could show up from a healthier and more balanced frame of mind but he was so resistant. He wasn't working out. He wasn't using the upgraded golf simulator in the garage he had to have. He wasn't doing anything outside of work, only helped a few nights a week to cook dinner with me, then always wrapped up the night with TV and cocktails.

He sat in silence. He looked at me and said, "Candice, I know you are going to think this is an excuse, but that violation of trust all those years back… I have never looked at you the same. I didn't want to walk away because of the kids and what people would think of me leaving the family. I felt like I didn't know you after that."

"Of course," I replied meeting him with understanding. In a gentle tone, I shared, "That sure would have been nice to know all these years. I have periodically brought this up to you and each time you reiterated that everything is fine. That you have forgiven me. Have moved on."

As he shared everything I felt terrible. I had been punishing myself for this for years because I respected him. And what I did was never about him. It was about me unhealed, living in fear, creating chaos in the moment because that was what felt safe. All I could do was understand his position and meet him with compassion, even though a part of me was angry he didn't share this earlier in our relationship.

He continued, "I have been unhappy for the past seven years and I am not in love or attracted to you."

What the fuck, I thought. Another blow to the gut. Keeping my composure, I felt a silent internal rage having just relocated, left my daughter, my kids' friends, school, and my kid's therapist for his special needs, sold the house and built a new one, and parted ways with the studio I had been working at... so much change, and this whole time he had been unhappy, not in love or attracted to me... for seven years.

"I thought before we left our last duty station everything had been put out on the table. Don't you think these details were important to share back then? You just uprooted all of us and you don't want to be with me."

"I know, I am sorry," he replied. Why had he left this huge detail out? I was sick to my stomach. And also, the last several years suddenly made sense. And then the belief, *I am not enough,* was watered once again.

We talked for so many hours. As fast as the day went by it felt like it was in slow motion, too. I cried so much. Staring out the window at the greenbelt, heart in pieces, tears streaming down my face, I wondered how we got here. Blaming myself again for my mistake all those years ago, it felt like it was fresh, like it had just happened. *Was I too hard to live with?* I asked myself in contemplation. My parents always told me I was a *good girl*, but when I messed up, I messed up big. I couldn't help but remember and reflect on that. So many questions came and went; some I asked, others I didn't. One question I had to ask about was my unattractiveness. I had dealt with judgment, criticism, and so much shaming on my looks and body my entire life, I needed to know. So I asked, "Keith, what is it that makes me unattractive?"

It took some work to get him to respond, as he was not an intentionally mean person. "You look masculine... you never do your hair, makeup, or get dressed up. And your weight gain over the years."

I don't have the words in my vocabulary to describe the feelings of inadequacy, shame, and "not enoughness" I felt after he said that. And as if this information wasn't enough to validate how I already felt about myself, I had to take it a step further. After a back and forth question, asking if it was my face, my body, or both, he clarified it was not my face that was unattractive but rather my body. Asking him if that was why he had not been intimate with me all these years, he confirmed this with a head nod.

I was distraught. *It's not my face, it's my body.*

Feeling so heartbroken, I couldn't help but express my feelings after hearing this. "You also are overweight, don't take care of yourself, wear sweats and T-shirts daily, are super toxic and hard to be around, drink daily, and you are telling me these things? How about courting me and taking me on a date so I have a reason to get dressed up?"

He was holding me to expectations and standards he was not willing to hold himself to. I was angry. I was crushed. *How was this happening?* I asked myself. *I knew it. How did I not listen to my intuition all these years?*

I spent the evening staring at myself in the mirror, seeing exactly why he was not attracted to me. Seeing all the flaws and imperfections, the scars, the stretch marks... I stared at myself in shame for not being pretty enough, for gaining all the weight, and not seeing what was right in front of me. I had been in denial for years. Clinging to hope that things would improve. Clinging to our potential. Clinging to prayers he would eventually want to seek healing.

The next morning I told him he needed to stay at a hotel for the week to really think about what he wanted. I didn't have much confidence but I knew I was never going to force someone to be with me. Like him all these years, I also put up with a lot, and I did it because I loved this man to death and that's what you do. But I was not going to continue losing time while he idled out of fear of judgment from his family.

Keith returned home on Friday after work. Sitting down, we had an open conversation to see what he had decided. His decision was to go to therapy, marriage counseling, and to make an appointment with a functional medicine team to get evaluated, and then go from there. I felt so happy because I knew all those things he mentioned would be so helpful to him, and eventually to us. There was a lot he was harboring and talking to someone could be so helpful. I also knew his health had taken a backseat for years, the drinking being a contributing factor.

Things seemed to get better. We celebrated our youngest's thirteenth birthday, and Keith even planned a couple weekend trips to go-karts and movies, which was a change from us sitting around the house watching TV all day. I felt like we were making small pivots that were going to stack upon one another, hopefully leading to big pivots and ultimately a healthier marriage.

I am no saint in this. I am sure I can be a lot to handle with all my heavy emotions, especially with someone who is not in touch with their own. I needed reassurance a lot over the last couple years, lately more than ever. But, it also felt like my basic needs in the relationship were not being met.

He got into therapy pretty quickly, and I was still actively engaged with my support team. We were both pretty focused on ourselves individually and then had open lines of communication to prevent any blindsiding. I was finally able to start breathing again and let my guard down just a little, as I had been on edge for what felt like weeks. Both of us were still not drinking and going to bed at decent times; I felt like we were off to a good start. He had his first intake appointment and felt really good about the therapist he was assigned. *Are brighter days ahead for us both?* I hoped.

I share this chapter, Reader, because I think many times in our life we hang onto someone or something because we fear the change of what comes along with losing it. We have built a familiarity, comfortableness, or safety in our system, regardless of its health, and the thought of change can be jolting to our system. I dismissed my intuition for years. I knew while overseas it was the beginning of the end. I won't sit in the victim seat any longer and blame him for what I felt was a lack of communication and effort on his part. I will own that I, too, felt disconnection for years and remained because of my guilt. And I could even go as far as to say staying was maybe a subconscious way to punish myself for my violation in the beginning. I was what cracked the foundation. We will never know what could have been, and this was exactly how it was supposed to play out for us each to get what we needed. You are divinely created with a deep knowing. The more trust you build with this beautifully created sacred vessel, the more you are living in tune with your true desires.

PERMISSION GRANTED to take the courageous steps needed to align with your truth and purpose.

The Emergence Era

"Some of our greatest storms are actually clearing away the debris so we can see our path clearly and bloom again."

—Candice West

Time continued to pass and some things changed, while others stayed the same... like how Keith spoke to the kids, watched TV all day, and made me feel invisible in a room sitting right next to him. One evening, fed up with it all, I took a deep breath and asked about the status of marriage counseling. Trying to give him space, things were not changing and I needed a pulse on his intentions... almost like my nervous system needed a timeline to know how much longer I would have to hold on.

"I didn't know we would be doing that right away. I thought I would spend time in therapy figuring myself out before starting marriage counseling," he shared.

I felt so confused. *Is this a genuine response or is he avoiding this part?* He happened to have a therapy appointment and while mentioning something about us, his therapist responded that it would be something discussed in marriage counseling. After his appointment he shared with me some key takeaways and that we needed to set something up. I spent some time later that day looking for someone knowledgeable of military life, internal family systems, trauma, autism, and blended families so we could get someone who would understand our family's dynamic. I was lucky enough to find someone locally who had an opening the following week.

We had an early morning marriage counseling intake call. I was anxious because I knew it was going to be hard work, but I also knew hard had been my life; if I had made it through all I had, I could do this, too. The counselor started off by explaining her role and how even through therapy some couples might find they are better going their separate ways. Keith's face lit up when she said that; it was like a permission slip he had hoped to hear. Then we dove right in. I went first answering the questions. I was honest and shared the real and raw truths I was harboring. Keith also shared in the exchanges, offering his real and raw truths. The next response Keith shared to the counselor would leave me with another blow to my stomach: "She has a lot of needs..." Suddenly my ears were ringing, tunnel vision set in, and everything around me went blank. I erupted. Tears... so many tears. Keith was still talking; as he noticed my face I could see a combination of both irritation and shock. As he finished his statement, the counselor stated, "Keith, correct me if I am wrong but when you said Candice had a lot of needs, I think what you meant to say was that she has a lot of needs you can't fill." He commented back in agreement, nodding his head yes. I was shut down at that point. Numb. Just done. Regardless of the statement and the reframe from the counselor, I took away two messages from that call: 1) I am too much and 2) He was not able to meet my needs. We finished the call and discussed what the following sessions would look like.

Afterwards, I laid on my office carpet floor sobbing. "Too much," I yelled. "Too much? I have been putting my needs aside for years to make everyone in this house happy!"

Late nights, sleep deprivation, no physical touch, sex, intimacy, connection, or courtship... nothing in so long. My voice stolen because he interrupted me constantly, overpowering the conversations when he wanted to make a point. So much so that I have also tolerated giving away my power. Gaslit and lied to for seven years. Him allowing me to think it was all me, him allowing me to own it all. I was irate. I was livid. I was angry. Both dogs now stood outside my French glass doors in protector mode.

I called Jennifer because I needed someone to talk to. I was confused, sad, feeling misunderstood, trying to wrap my head around what was happening. She offered her ear, her knowledge, her support. My pilates bestie came over shortly afterward to just listen and hold space for me. That day was a blur, but it was what was needed for it all to come out. This was the final piece. The last part he had not shared over the many talks we'd had in the recent year.

Later that day, Keith had a therapy appointment. When he got home nothing was mentioned about earlier to avoid disruption in the house. We tended to the animals and the kids, made dinner, and cleaned up for the night. We both headed to bed at a decent hour, which seemed to be our new normal now that we were no longer drinking. We gave each other space and just acknowledged to ourselves that the day had been a hard one.

I was deep in my retreat planning as I was about two weeks away from my first in-person women's weekend retreat. I was working on a lot—last-minute decisions, swag bags, decor, all the little details that add to the clients' experience. I happened to check all the things off my to-do list and was sitting in the Target parking lot when my afternoon client canceled at the last minute. I thought, *Okay, well, there is that local ranch on social media that I have been wanting to go see… maybe today is the perfect day. After all, I am already out and about. It's a beautiful sunny day, 1:30 p.m., so why not?* I loaded the address into the GPS and it had an arrival time of 2:22 p.m.—the "angel number" that represents balance, harmony, and spiritual alignment. *No way! Umm yes, this is a sign. No questions or thinking any further; I am going,* I told myself. So off I went to this random location out in the boonies to see this ranch I knew nothing about but felt pulled to go to. Sounds about as Candice as it gets.

As I pulled into the ranch I saw all the different flags representing the United States military branches of service. I was immediately pulled in. I slowly drove through their curvy driveway, making my way toward the fence lines that were full of beautiful horses. I couldn't help but drive slowly to capture all their pretty faces, notice their different colors, and observe them in their essence. It reminded me of the horse, named Carrie, we'd had at my grandparents' for a short period of time. I kept driving back and happened to see a house and a couple big barns. Unsure where to park, I kept going forward, which brought me to a paved area with another parked car. Parking the car I looked around for a moment to notice the pasture, all the animals, and the smell. I took it all in! *Wow, this is beautiful,* I thought.

I got out of my car and looked around to see if I could see anyone when an older gentleman came out of the barn. I got his attention and asked if the person in charge was around. Just as he started talking to me the owner started walking in our direction. The gentlemen introduced me to the owner and let us connect while he wandered off, finishing his task. The owner and I started chatting, and she told me about their work and mission. I learned they offer respite for wounded warriors and their families. It is a place they can spend the weekend to connect, rest, and interact with all the animals for healing. I was so inspired.

She took me into her office to show me various programs she offered and said she had an interest in collaborating with me on some future workshops. I was so excited! This seemed perfect. *This is why I was meant to come today*, I thought. As we continued talking she asked if I wanted to look at all the animals. We made our way out to the pasture and fence line. I started to notice all the animals moving toward the fence. Like, all of them. Every single one of them. The owner commented on how they must like me because they were all coming in my direction. I had a ginormous smile on my face. How cute they all were. Horses, ponies, goats, donkeys, dogs, cats, all coming from different fence lines to the edge.

As I stood there taking them all in, the owner began telling me a little more about their animals. She shared how all the animals at the ranch were surrendered. They were rescues. She explained that each of these pets had different owners who were unable to care for them because they didn't realize the work that comes with owning pets. They ended up being too much, so they abandoned them or surrendered them. *Candice, you got this. Inhale .... hold ... exhale ... hold,* I told myself. Ya'll, the lump in my throat was fierce. She continued to share that she and her spouse had taken each and every one of these animals into their possession and cared for them with so much love. She shared how much joy they have brought to their lives and the lives of all the volunteers and guests. Paying attention to time, I knew I needed to start heading back. I thanked her for her time and told her I looked forward to connecting and collaborating soon.

I got into my car and barely made it halfway down the driveway before I broke into tears. Each of these pets had owners that deemed them as *too much*. But yet, this couple brought each and every one of them into their home and hearts and cared for them just as they are. In that now moment I heard so clearly, "Candice, you are not too much; you are too much for the wrong person."

I gasped, realizing that was the reason I was pulled to go to the ranch. I needed to see that one owner can struggle to meet the needs of one horse, and also, one owner can supply enough love to an entire ranch. This blew my mind and made me realize the marriage counselor had it right. It wasn't that I was too needy and too much; it was just that Keith was not able to meet my needs. *Is this a sign that he is never going to be able to meet me where I am now? Had I healed so much we were no longer compatible?* So many thoughts ran rampant through my mind during that forty-five-minute car ride home.

I arrived home in time to fix my face, drink some water, use the restroom, and log onto the call. It was just the pick-me-up I needed... ladies chatting, getting amped about the upcoming event. We hung up from our call, and then I made my way to the living room. Keith made his way upstairs from the basement and we found ourselves again in deep conversation. But this time, he started it.

"Candice, I had a stressful day at work and I wanted to unwind and not take it out on anyone so I went down to the basement to play video games. Broc came downstairs to ask what was for dinner, and I snapped at him."

Now, this was his usual behavior toward the kids... always on edge and bothered when the kids needed something. Keith told me he'd lashed out at him and then afterward felt bad because he had not communicated to anyone that he needed this time alone.

Now in full dialogue, Keith continued sharing that earlier in the week following our marriage counseling appointment he'd had his own personal therapy appointment. He had shared with his therapist something that happened in the house, to which the therapist responded (Keith paraphrasing), "I am surprised to hear that is how you handled that. When we had our last call you shared a similar story, only it was your parents who treated you that way. It appears that you are repeating the same patterns." After Keith shared that I could see his eyes well up. I felt the presence of shame in his energy. He continued to share but his deepest take away was that he was treating the children in a way he didn't like, and that was not okay with him. I will say it was frustrating to hear him acknowledge and accept that truth when I had been communicating that to him for years. And, I felt a deep compassion for him and appreciation for his transparency.

Keith proceeded to ask about my day. I felt an awkwardness fill my internal cavity, knowing it would bring up even more. I knew I couldn't make it about him. I needed to be true to myself regardless of the outcome. It was an energy of detaching and allowing all in the same big breath. And so I shared. I shared every piece of that message, what it meant to me, and what it revealed. I could see his body shift as I shared. I loved this man to death, so I was willing to go to the depths to get us back on track. I really could see it... we just needed some support. Again, I reminded myself it was my anxious attachment style and his avoidant attachment style, and all we needed to do was learn how to support one another moving through our struggles. We needed to stay the course with marriage counseling to learn how to navigate through this with each other.

That's when he revealed our season was over. Our chapter as Keith and Candice no longer made sense. It felt like all I had done this far into the new year was cry, scream, repeat. The story, *all men leave me*, was being watered once again, playing loudly and on repeat in my mind. We sat there in silence for quite some time. We headed to bed and for the first time in a long time I prayed. I prayed to God, telling him how awful he was. The questions I had asked so many times before played on repeat in my head until I finally fell asleep.

The next morning I headed to the hair salon for my appointment. I hadn't slept well, had a headache and puffy red eyes, and was nauseous. The weather matched my mood... gloomy and a torrential downpour. This hair appointment was so odd. I had sat in her chair many times before, but today, she shared how she was going through a divorce and how terrible her spouse was acting. I remember thinking, *Oh no, I don't have it in me for another tumultuous breakup.* That had been all I'd ever known from childhood and my other two serious relationships. I couldn't do it again. I listened to her story and also thought, *This is nowhere near the same. Why are we separating?* It gave me a lot to think about and consider, but one thing was for certain: I loved this man deep to my core.

I got home and Keith shared that while I was gone he went apartment searching. He was able to find an affordable one with availability to move in the following week. I thought to myself, *Man, he didn't waste any time. If only he had moved this fast to seek personal and marriage therapy, then where could we be?* My heart sank again. What do you say to that, *Thank you? Okay? Sounds good?* The boys were home, so all I could do was acknowledge his wishes and show him the respect he deserved for taking a step in the direction to find his happiness.

At this point we were in planning mode… we needed a plan since he would be moving out in just a handful of days. Not only did I need to process this all, we needed to tell the kids something. So many thoughts filled my head… *What about marriage counseling—is that still happening? We just bought this house—do we sell? You just relocated us here away from my daughter—do I go back?* I was absolutely crushed. My mind circled the drain of all the beliefs that had been growing over the years. All these beliefs that lived awake and inside my body were causing him to walk away from me and our family. I made it about me. I blamed myself for my mistake years prior. For seven years I'd tried so hard; I did the healing work, I dug into myself so I could be better not only for me, but for my kids and our marriage. None of it was good enough.

We spent that Saturday evening drafting a plan to tell the kids. Nattie went first—she was devastated, of course, triggering her own abandonment wound she still carried from her father. She feared that Keith would also exit her life and she would lose the man who had always been there for her. The man who helped her through her first period while I was deployed. The man who hugged her when her ex-boyfriend did her dirty. The man who planned a small prom for her in our apartment tower overseas during the pandemic so she didn't miss out. The man who was black and white, blunt and to the point, and always told her what she needed to hear versus what she wanted to hear.

We called the boys downstairs to share the news. They both thought it was an early April Fool's joke, which crushed me. When my face shifted and Keith reiterated what he had already said, I could see tears rolling down Zander's face. Broc sat there staring at the floor with patchy red blotches on his face and neck, telling us he was fine. Both verbalized being confused and just didn't understand what was happening. Funny, I was also in that same energy and in denial at the same time.

Sunday made for a long day. I sat for hours frozen on the couch, staring out the window into the backyard greenbelt. Zander shared with me he wanted to go to his dad's house so I booked a hotel for a few nights because, honestly, I needed some alone time to process without Keith and the kids. We loaded up the car, and Zander and I headed out.

I used this opportunity to journal. I journaled so much. I cried and cried over and over. I danced in the hotel room, moving my energy and the heaviness of my emotions. I would meet moments of certainty that this was in fact the right move, then I would crumble, wondering how on earth I was going to let go of all this time together—the memories, the love. It felt like someone was ripping out my insides. Lying in the bed frozen, I thought to myself, *This is my punishment. My punishment for the times in life I was unfaithful, a homewrecker, a side piece. For all the times I lied because that is what felt safest in the moment. For the names I called my mom and being no-contact. For killing my dad.* My head went down every single rabbit hole, looking for all the ways to punish myself.

Journal Entry

God, why are you doing this to me again? Why are you stripping me down bare, expecting me to start over? I am trying so hard to trust and have faith but I can't find it. I am struggling here to understand what you're doing. I suppose this isn't for me to make sense of. We each are on a journey and that looks different for us both. But why couldn't you have let us do this together?

I also felt spurts of anger. I had no parents to call or to cry to. I felt alone. I knew I needed to process this myself. I knew this was my next layer to healing. My next challenge to rewire old patterns of self-soothing. So remaining committed to myself, using the tools in my program and others I had created along my healing journey, I began identifying all the parts that were resurfacing in that now moment. I welcomed them all in one by one: the people-pleaser, the over-thinker, the depressed, the controller, all of them. I needed to understand what they were, why they were still there, and how I could witness them in that now moment. What did they need? When and why were they birthed to begin with? The next couple days were awful. The pain I felt is indescribable. I wouldn't wish it on anyone. Everything kept cycling in my mind ....

I am not good enough.

I am too fat.
I am not pretty enough.
I am too needy.
All men leave me.
All men hurt me.
Men are not safe.

I felt so much anger toward Keith, too. It is his God-given birthright to be happy, and if I was not his happy I wanted him to go find his happiness. I loved him enough to let him go. I was still furious that for seven years he was unhappy and never verbally mentioned it, even when asked. Years I fought so hard for us. Years I was being manipulated because he was fearful to step forward. In those moments I remember thinking how he stole seven years of my life, years I will never get back.

I would catch my breath, feel a bit of peace in his decision, and then the next thought would surface: *I am unattractive.* I was so angry he never mentioned or brought up concerns about my looks. *Can a sister get a heads up before you just up and leave? What happened to unconditional love? I have grown three children full term, had multiple surgeries, experienced lifelong trauma — what do you expect me to look like?* I thought I had scored a man. A real man who loved me unconditionally. I was wrong.

Zander decided he wanted to stay a little longer with his dad so I headed home. It was a peaceful and reflective drive; I decided I would leave again Friday, spending the weekend at the hotel with Broc. I knew he would be resistant to leaving, but I wanted to get him out of the house, since Keith would be moving out. I didn't want us to have to witness that. It was too much, too soon. I thought the oceanfront with Saint Patrick's Day events could be really fun and just what we needed. I also wanted Keith to have his privacy and didn't want him feeling guilty for doing what he felt he needed to do.

Broc and I checked into the hotel and enjoyed our time together. Once we had Zander back with us the following day, we spent the time at the beach walking, eating, playing, and even processing.

"Mom, you really know how to blow through men," one of my boys said as he was trying to make sense of this unexpected news. Driving in the car, all I could say was, "Yeah, seems like it, buddy." How do you respond to a statement like that? I was so hurt hearing that; I cried, staring forward so he wouldn't see me. We got back to the hotel, and I walked right into the bathroom. You know those cries where it all wants to erupt, come to the surface, but because of where you are or who you are around you have to stifle it? I stood in the bathroom, hands on the edges of the bathroom sink, doing exactly that. I didn't want him to feel bad, and also, I felt bad. They both had so many questions I couldn't answer, I had to start keeping a list. This was such a hard part of the process. My first divorce, Nattie was so small, so I didn't have to answer questions. She went to bed early so I could wait it out until she fell asleep. This time was different.

The weekend was over, and we were headed back to the house. It was so weird arriving and being alone. I knew immediately I needed to create a new flow, a healthy routine to help me navigate processing my emotions while also holding space for the boys, managing our 4,200-square-foot home, caring for our four animals, and running my business. This was our new beginning.

The reality of this chapter? Courage. Keith had a courage I didn't have even when deep down the writing was on the wall. The message was clear to me, and yet, as he shared our season was over, I just couldn't accept it. You see, Reader, as much as it was the sadness of our season ending, it was even more about the deep-seated wounding from childhood that had been activated in his decision making. The rejection, the not-enoughness, the belief that all men leave me. I allowed his realization of his unhappiness within our partnership to reinforce the internal stories that I was less than, when in fact, I am imperfectly perfect, just no longer a match for and with him. Be gentle with yourself if you have been on either side of this story. Allow your inner-child to be held. Give yourself some space and some love. Life is a giant test, and we are all here learning as we go.

PERMISSION GRANTED to release old beliefs and embrace your present truth with compassion and clarity.

The Me Era

"Your greatest self has been waiting your whole life;
don't make it wait any longer."
—Dr. Steve Maraboli

The next couple months were incredibly heavy, hard, and healing. I integrated journaling into my day. I allowed myself to write whatever surfaced, not labeling it as right, wrong, good, bad, true, or untrue. I moved my body; I cried, yelled, and screamed. I had long, hard talks over the phone with Keith, pouring my heart out, crying, and sometimes yelling in anger and disappointment. He was always so understanding, and yet, nothing ever came from him. I was not sure if he was so over me and so relieved to finally be free that he was unfazed. But it hurt to not see him affected. And also, that seemed to be how he presented in our relationship all those years—distant and disconnected.

We decided selling the house was best. We had come to Virginia to support him in his career but none of us had wanted to move. Now in this position of separation, did we really need to stay? Just a couple hours away was a location where I was stationed for twelve years, where Zander's dad lived, where I could have a flourishing business, and where I had a familiar support system. Though the kids were not thrilled to be a new kid again, they saw the bigger picture. Zander was also excited to be closer to his dad. Keith took the news well; he figured we would not want to remain where we were, and I couldn't afford living there unless I got a typical nine to five job, which I did not desire to do after all I had invested in my own business.

I took quick action to map the sale and purchase of a new house, move the family, and be set up to be able to still do all the traveling I had already planned for the summer while still working on my business goals. That is one thing about me I admire... I move best under pressure. I move quickly, intelligently, and intentionally. These two months were a roller coaster. They were peaks and valleys. There were days I felt solid and knew to my core this was the right move, then other days and nights I grieved and grieved for hours at a time. There were days I cried all day on the couch. I chose not to hide this part of me. To show the boys what heavy emotions, feelings, and processing grief looked like. And most importantly, that it was okay to feel. I didn't want them dissociating and hiding but rather witnessing through my actions a permission slip to feel all the feels... sadness, anger, frustration. All of it was welcome.

I was still alcohol-free, binge-eating-free, and not seeking male attention elsewhere. I was fucking proud of myself. This was the first time in my life I was not looking for love somewhere other than self. This was the first time I was treating my body as a sacred vessel. The work I had been doing all these years, especially in the recent six months, was all paying off. I was breaking the patterns that had been passed down intergenerationally.

I happened to go back down to the Hampton Road area to meet with my realtor, Racheal, who also happened to be a friend from when I was stationed there previously. We had picked out a handful of houses to look at to potentially place an offer on the following week when my house was listed. I met her on a Friday evening and toured a new neighborhood that was planted in a great school district. I immediately fell in love with the color, the layout, and the community but was also concerned at the price point. After touring that community, I headed back to the hotel to unwind and journal. As I laid there with my mind circling, I wondered how to pick. *How do I decide which it is?* As I drifted off to sleep, I prayed to God asking for a sign. "God, I need a sign. This is too much all at the same time to process and decide. What if I make the wrong decision and the boys are miserable? What if I buy a house and it falls apart in six months?" I typically went for a feather as a sign because that's the connection I have with my dad. But I knew I would likely see feathers everywhere because of the time of year, so that would only lead to more overthinking. I didn't want to overthink a sign. What came next was odd for me; it was not something I typically thought of. *A cardinal.* I told myself if I saw a cardinal on the way to a house I was viewing or in a house I was viewing, that, no questions asked, that's the house I would choose.

Racheal and I met up first thing in the morning and got started. She had five houses for me to look at that I'd picked and were at my price point. We went to each house, but nothing felt like home. As we wrapped up looking at all the houses I asked Racheal if we could go back and look at the new construction home from the day prior. We drove back to look at this other house and wouldn't you know it, a cardinal zipped off to the right of my vehicle. "Nuh-uh! No way! A cardinal. I just saw a cardinal!" I shouted to myself.

Tears filled my eyes. I felt so held and carried, so emotional in that moment. I felt this feeling overwhelm my body, saying, *You don't have to do this alone.* Feeling so connected, comforted, and more confident, we got to the house and I looked around. I allowed myself to feel into the space as Racheal and the sales rep from the building company chatted. I envisioned my boys there, the animals there, me there. I envisioned what I could do with my business there. I envisioned how I felt there... this felt like home. This was it.

I immediately told Racheal I wanted to make an offer. I rushed to contact my agent and informed her I'd found something I didn't want to lose. "Could we list my house today?" I asked her. To my luck, the photos and videos we had taken of the house the previous days were ready and it was only a matter of time. My realtor was on it! In just a few hours she had my house listed and opened for scheduled viewings. And within an hour and a half after she listed my home I had numerous requests to tour the space. So many that she ended up converting the following day, Easter Sunday, into an open house, which typically was not done since it was a holiday. I immediately contacted Keith, informing him of this impromptu open house and that he would need to take the kids and animals to his apartment. I couldn't believe it. Everything was falling into place so rapidly, as if this was what was always meant to be.

The open house was successful, actually going over its scheduled time by an hour. By that evening there were five offers all over the asking price with different additional options based on the timing I wanted to physically leave the house. I remember thinking, *Oh my gosh, this clearly is how it is all supposed to be happening.* Sitting in the energy of all of this happening for me, for us, I started to realize I shouldn't be questioning what or why things were happening but feel gratitude for it all instead. Everything happens for a reason. When I look back over my life and see how things have unfolded, the blessings I have received through darkness and heartache, it makes me wonder why I ever question anything at all.

We accepted an offer on the house and had a closing date of June 1. That date wouldn't even be ninety days from my and Keith's separation. It is crazy how fast things can unfold and life can change. Tuesday morning after the observed holiday, Racheal was on the phone with the builder, letting them know I had an official offer on my house. Being a new month, the incentives the builder was originally offering were no longer valid. Racheal went hard for me, and long story short, I was able to get the house at a price I could afford. Within that evening I received the documents and was officially under contract. *What? How did this all happen so fast?* Well, it does when it is God, Source, Universe's plan.

Sitting in my living room in tears, Zander came downstairs to see me crying. "Mom, I am sorry you are sad. It's okay to cry," he told me. It felt good to share with him that the tears flowed not out of sadness but out of gratitude and appreciation. I sat in the energy, allowing myself to celebrate me and how I was handling all I was being faced with in such a short amount of time. Still alcohol-free, still focused on my nutrition, still making sure I moved, for the first time in my life it was all about me. I had entered my #meera.

Through my healing process and grieving process I realized I was attached to the potential of us. To the way I knew we could be as a couple if we could work on our challenges both individually and as a couple. But I also started realizing I could not force it on him. He had to be the one who wanted to do *the work*. To want to heal. And through this process, I realized that while there was grief of what I thought our future would look like, what our time once the kids were grown would look like, what retirement life would look like, it was also the purging of all the beliefs that had been planted, watered, and overtaking my body throughout my lifespan. The seeds of not enough, too much, too needy, unlovable... all of them were being pulled out one by one with each tear, scream, shout, yell, and sob session. That is why it was so painful. It was a love woven so deep, entangled and enmeshed with deeply rooted beliefs that were not serving me. It was a beautiful unraveling. A beautiful realization. Realizing that it was him... he was my gift to healing so many years of trauma. He was my gift to truly seeing myself as the sacred vessel I was. Had he never left, had he not had the courage to put himself first, to choose himself, I would never have faced these beliefs and excavated them at the depth I did. They would have continued to entangle his love, our love, sabotaging the potential I could see for us. It was never his job to make me happy. It was never his job to reassure me. It was never his job to do things I needed... *it was my job*. His efforts should have reinforced and complemented what I already felt within. But instead, I relied on him and all those things to make me feel valued, accepted, and worthy. What an impossible feat. It was what I had done my entire life in almost all of my relationships.

Now in the mode of preparing to move and get the new house all ready, I found myself next-level stressed out. I had forgotten how hard it was being a single mom. It was not just about trying to learn how to cook again, since that was Keith's forte. It was all the house chores, all the animals, all of it in that large home. I went through bouts of anger, launching ice cubes into the shower, punching my son's punching bag, envisioning the faces of the people in my life who had let me down to process and discharge all the energy versus tucking it away somewhere within. I found myself randomly crying, hearing a song that would bring me back to a moment in time. Thinking about holidays and everyone being divided. I also started to feel some resentment. Keith's responsibility consisted of going to work then coming home to play video games. *Tough life*, I thought to myself. *You leave us and I am left to clean up all this shit while you get to escape. Nice plan, dude.* I found myself feeling like I wanted to punch him when I saw him in those moments because it just felt so unfair.

I allowed myself time in the victim seat. It was needed, it was warranted. But I never chose to remain there. I typically would shift rather quickly from the victim mentality to one of self-empowerment. And it wasn't toxic positivity—trust me, I processed. It was one of the biggest reasons I reminded myself daily I was so thankful I'd listened to my full body in signing up for my program. It was *the work* that was allowing me and giving me permission to show up in a way that truly felt aligned and as an example I would want to demonstrate to my kids. There were times I felt empowered to call Keith and unload, as he welcomed it. Other times, it was a personal, very sacred process. My body had been through enough, and I no longer subscribed to tucking it all away. I no longer subscribed to pretending to protect my kids. My #meera was welcoming it all.

Moving day was here; another new beginning was among us. I was met with sadness in the morning. I loved this house. It was a true labor of love. I stood in each room remembering me and Keith decorating the walls on the weekend after we moved in, hanging the the contact paper in my office, painting the spare rooms, and sitting outside on the back porch staring off into the greenbelt at the deer, bunnies, squirrels, even wild turkeys. Oh, how I would miss this feeling, this peacefulness and serenity this place brought me even during all the chaos. The colors of the leaves changing come fall, the birds chirping as if they were answering my prayers. But it was time to move on. As my friend, Jennifer, said, "You've struggled building your in-person business here because you were never meant to stay." What a surprise and gift she was. Listening to the wisdom within had found me a new love for pilates but also a friend and sister for life, the biggest gift. One I would have never been in receipt of had I not listened to the nudge and walked through the door.

Planting new roots in Chesapeake, growing our new life here, felt good. It felt clean, energetically. Better than I thought it would. Keith offered to stay with us the first weekend to help us get all settled. Honestly, I didn't know how I felt about it and battled myself wanting to be independent and not having to rely on him for help. "Mom, Dad helping get our rooms situated is for us, to help us get settled, not you." Zander, a wise one speaking truth, served as that reminder that help didn't mean I was weak, that I couldn't do all these things myself, but rather, someone was extending help so I didn't have to do it all myself. Noted, son… wish granted. Keith stayed in the guest room and honestly, he helped so much. By the end of the weekend when he headed back I was just about unpacked and the garage was organized, dimmers installed, pendant lights swapped out, ceiling fans installed, and electronics all connected and set up. Whether it was for us or to ease some of the guilt he was battling didn't matter to me; it was much appreciated and helped with our transition.

My #meera was unfamiliar. I was doing things on my own terms. Watching TV shows I wanted to watch. Or no TV at all and listening to music as I journaled or worked on my business. Buying what foods I wanted to buy. Doing laundry on a Wednesday instead of the mandatory Sunday. Grocery shopping on a Tuesday instead of the mandatory Sunday. The rules for the kids were my say-so. I wasn't being interrupted, muted, or corrected for how I wanted to do things with them. I let them speak, even if the answer was no, to give them their sense of self and power. And to support their voice so they learned to communicate and develop their own personal authority.

It wasn't long before the boys were sharing how different it was. One even said, "Mom, this feels like home. I am happy here." The other said, "Mom, it feels more peaceful here. Like, there's a lot more laughter." And then countless times where they would make a mistake and then guard themselves, awaiting the nasty, condescending, belittling remark. It was sad to witness as a mother because I saw it and I didn't, if that even makes sense. My sister, Jennifer, helped me make it make sense. She said, "You built a tolerance over the years living with Mom and Dad, so what was happening in your home wasn't glaringly obvious until the end." She said it perfectly.

Journal Entry

The moment you realize you have been relying on your relationships to bring you joy and happiness is the moment you realize you have been giving away your own power.

After Keith left, I lost ten pounds in a month... and that's not because I wasn't eating. I sat in the noticing and curiosity of it all, and some profound truths immediately came over me.

- I believe my body was holding onto the toxic environment.
- My body had been holding onto the shame of my mistakes.
- My own self-destructive habits were a way to punish myself for all I had done wrong.
- My own self-sabotaging behaviors were a way for my body to remain safe and held.
- Bad things happen to me when I look my best.
- I have done bad things when I looked my best.
- My body was in self-protection mode.

So much began to change within as time passed. My inflammation was better, my joints felt better, I slept so much better. Everyone was thriving, including Keith.

I began considering, *What does life look like for Candice? Pulling out the kids, pulling out what it should look like, what is it that I desire?* I made a list of what sparks joy for me. The things that lit me up. And as the days went by I started checking them off one by one. I started dating myself, so much so that I took myself to a Morgan Wallen concert and had an absolute blast. This self-dating continues even today. I sit on my back porch gazing at the sun and stars in full awe that I have freedoms that I have never experienced. I go to the pool in a swimsuit and walk around not giving a flying fuck who is looking at me and my cellulite. I come and go for no rhyme or reason, welcoming what experience it brings me—*spontaneity*, oh how I crave it. I am playing with my hairstyle, hair color, and even makeup looks, because I don't feel obligated to have to look a certain way. I am decorating my house considering whether I like it or not, not what is trending. I even took a leap in my business and booked a media production with photography in Colorado as part of my book launch. I stay up late, sleep in, and am even trying new foods without the judgment of having to waste it because it is awful. I even learned how to cook (it counts even though it's an air fryer, right?).

What I have been learning in this #meera is that I am a pretty incredible person: funny, smart, witty, creative, and fun. I am loving, compassionate, full of grace, and sincere. My strength, resilience, and personal power have no place in this. Those things no longer matter to me. It was a given I was and am all those things. What I needed to discover, learn, and believe was that there was more to me than all that. I had been applauded my whole life for being strong and adaptable, but it was forced. I no longer desire to be connected or associated with those roles because of my situations. I was all of this without indulging in food, restricting food, drinking alcohol, immersing myself in men, seeking attention outside of self, and obsessing over my appearance and looks. I was learning there was so much more to Candice. Oh hi, nice to meet you, nice to meet me.

As I prepared for my Colorado event, in the weeks leading up to it I started noticing a theme in my daily life. I noticed the people-pleasing challenges arising in varying scenarios, providing me with the opportunity to stand in my truth, recognizing and naming my needs or choosing to succumb to old patterns. I chose me each and every time. I was taught at a very young age that having needs was too much. I was high-maintenance, I was an inconvenience, so much so that I stopped speaking about my own needs and just ensured the needs of those around me were met. Sometimes I wonder if that is where Caregiver Candice was born.

I started noticing things. I noticed where I felt it in my body. I noticed my thoughts. I noticed the belief that had been watered over the years and how much it had grown into so much more. I shared all these discoveries with my production team as they would be there to help guide me, support me, and reinforce the intention of it all. I felt extremely held and also like God had intentionally placed these people directly in my path. *Old Man might know what he's doing after all.* Since Keith moved out I had started feeling myself get pulled back to praying at night before bed. Praying that he would watch over me and help guide me. Praying that he would put his hand over all my kids, even Keith, to help them through these tough waters. Funny how I went from exiling God, to being angry with him, to calling out to him, and to finally trusting in him.

To the one who places everyone's needs before their own. To the one who feels uncomfortable saying no. To the one who feels tension in their body, ask yourself the simple but powerful question: *Who am I?* To the one who no longer knows who they are, I see you, I witness you, I was, and, in some cases, still am you. If this chapter opened something inside of you—a deep resonation—and if you could see yourself in even a paragraph, it's time to come home to self. It's time to join the #mereramovement; I welcome you.

PERMISSION GRANTED to reconnect with your true self and celebrate the process of coming home to who you are.

The Evolution Era

"Evolution is the law of nature, but what human beings
evolve into is 100 percent in our hands."

—Rishav

It was time. Production time, that is. Keith arrived on
Sunday to get settled into my home since he would be
watching the boys while I was away in Colorado. I spent the
evening steaming dresses, packing, and getting together all
the various things I needed to bring along. As the night
progressed I could feel the knots in my stomach. I knew
what I was setting out to do and I was determined to do it,
regardless of the nerves and fears that surfaced. This was a
moment for me to not only jump head first into my
evolution but to clear away and pull up deeply rooted
beliefs that had been in my system for as long as I can
remember. This was my chance to truly see myself for the
first time. I was scared shitless, to be honest. What if I didn't
like what I saw, literally and figuratively? I knew I was
going to be held, I knew I was going to be supported, and I
knew I had to be true to myself and the vision I had.
Alongside the supportive team, I had me. I had been
building my capacity and threshold for months. It was all
preparing me for those now moments. A true test of self; as
if the recent months prior hadn't already been a testament
to my ability to hold myself. I hopped into bed after telling

everyone goodnight and found myself just lying there. *Seriously*, I thought. *I have to be up in just a few hours. I need to sleep.* I tossed and turned until the alarm went off just a few hours later.

Three hours of sleep—*Sure. I have done this plenty of times as a mother of three. I'll sleep on the plane*, I said to myself. Quietly getting myself ready and loading the car, I headed to Norfolk International Airport with a large suitcase, carry-on suitcase, backpack, and my childhood violin. My short arms managed to haul it all in, checking the larger pieces, and then navigating my way to security. I got through security and found myself sitting in the Starbucks guzzling water and a turkey, cheddar, and egg-white muffin. I kept thinking with each bite, *Oh my gosh, today is the day. I am really doing this.* I headed over to an empty gate and sat strumming my violin like a guitar as I followed along to the app I was using for my music. I played so many variations, and I could feel the energy and emotions already moving in me.

I realized after several looks that the clock kept reading the same time. *Oh shoot! What time is it?* I managed to find another clock and it was 7:30 a.m.—we were supposed to start boarding in ten minutes. See, I couldn't even accidentally miss the flight! I used the restroom and headed over to the gate where I then boarded the plane. As I stepped beyond the agent where she scanned my ticket, I noticed heavy sensations in my body. I could feel my heart racing and my breathing getting rapid but shallow. I thought, *This is weird. What is happening? I don't mind flying.* Then it dawned on me. I was terrified for Colorado! I stood there taking step by step as they loaded people in front of me. I kept telling myself, *Candice, you're good. You're solid.*

You have this. You know what to do. This is fear of the unknown. This is fear of visibility at its highest level. I took deep breaths while looking through a small gap between the plane and the gate. My chest felt heavier and heavier and then I was next. I had a moment where I paused. My foot midstep, I reminded myself that by doing this work I, too, am healing my kids. The next instant my foot firmly planted onto the plane as I exhaled deeply.

I was lucky enough to get a window seat so after three-and-a-half hours of sleep I was looking forward to a nap. As I got all settled in and the cabin was secure and ready for takeoff, I suddenly felt the urge to use the restroom. *Nooooo,* I thought to myself. *Not already. I can't be that person asking the people next to me to get up. We are barely even in the air.* I immediately felt like a problem. I felt like they were going to be so annoyed with me already asking them to get up for a *potty break.* There was absolutely no way I was going to get up so I sat there and held it. About thirty minutes went by, and I saw the gentlemen in the aisle seat start to drift off. I thought, *Well, if I go now, then they can sleep the rest of the flight. If I wait then I risk having to wake him up.* I battled myself, then thought, *If I were in the aisle seat would I be sitting here or on the toilet?* I immediately recognized I was dismissing my own needs to avoid potentially making someone else uncomfortable or inconvenienced. *Ahhhh, Candice, you're doing it again, sacrificing self.*

I reminded myself in that moment that this was a basic human function, and with my bladder issues and urinary incontinence, did I really want to risk my hygiene and comfort over an assumption someone would be annoyed? "Hi, I am so sorry to be that person, but I actually need to use the restroom. So sorry to interrupt you," I said with an awkward smile to the lady next to me. "No problem, I actually wouldn't mind standing with the long flight ahead," she said, also with a smile. The gentleman, also very friendly, acknowledged me with another smile. If they were annoyed they did a great job hiding it!

After returning from the restroom I celebrated myself for speaking up and meeting my needs even when it was uncomfortable for me. I also realized that the reason I felt so uneasy about speaking up was because I was projecting my own personal reactions into the situation. Truth is, if I had been in either of those seats, and we had just taken off, I likely would have been annoyed to have to pack up my laptop and my headset, shut the tray table, and get up for my neighbor to go to the bathroom. So while, yes, I didn't want to inconvenience them, I was also assuming they would be inconvenienced because that's how I personally would have felt. *Ew,* I thought. It was an immediate opportunity for me to make note of how I felt so in the future, I could present with a warm smile.

I slept through most of the flight, disembarked, and finally arrived at the hotel. I headed to my room and began unpacking those dresses I now had to steam again since they had been folded up in the luggage. I sat on the bed for a few moments and decided to journal because I just felt so full, excited, nervous; so many feelings flooded my body I needed to separate to see what, if anything, was hiding. I didn't want any surprises on set the next day.

To kick off my Colorado adventure, I would be meeting up with someone I had followed on social media for at least ten years and really admired. When she learned I was going to be in town she said she wanted to connect for coffee or lunch. Being a foodie, I am always down for a good meal. I arrived at the restaurant and we connected. She greeted me with a big hug and we headed to our table. We sat and chatted over lunch about our book processes, my media production, my lookbook (vision, outfits, intention) and life updates. It was nice hearing her feedback about what I was doing and some ideas that had been floating around in my mind. I must add, it is pretty inspiring when two women can get together, have honest and open dialogue, and leave wishing each other nothing but the best. I haven't always felt that in my sisterhood connections over the years. But, that is the kind of sisterhood I want to immerse myself in. More, please! This lunch was just what I needed to ground myself and ready myself for what the next couple days were going to bring.

Getting back to my room, all I could think about was a bath. I scrubbed out the tub and then pulled the plug and started the water. After a few minutes I realized the water was draining. Fumbling around, I realized the drain must be broken. I contemplated just taking a shower and saying to hell with the bath. But in that moment I paused and realized, *No, no, I want a bath.* I wrapped myself up in a towel and called down to the front desk. They were sending someone right up. I got dressed and waited for the knock on the door. The maintenance guy worked for ninety minutes and had to completely replace the drain plug with a manual one. What kept crossing my mind was how an older version of me would have just said forget it and compromised what I wanted and took a shower instead. But me in this #meera and #evolutionera knew I not only desired a bath, but I needed to follow through on this in order to rewire my patterns. I needed to stop minimizing and dismissing every need in order to please and accommodate everyone else. I also couldn't help but notice these situations arising back to back as I prepared for my experience. It felt empowering and liberating to follow through.

Sitting in the warm water, body wash used to replace bath bubbles, this bath was everything I needed. As I soaked in the water, thinking about where I was, all I had been through, and what I was about to embark on led me right into a somatic release. With violin music playing in the background, I found myself crying and crying and crying, not even being able to place a finger on the why. But at this point in my training and healing I knew *the what* and *the why* is irrelevant—it is *the release* that matters.

Feeling refreshed, I pulled out the dresses, accessories, and shoes I would need for day one of production, which was going to be held in the studio. I spent the next little bit of time steaming them all while envisioning myself in them, moving in them, smiling in them, and just embracing what this new version of self looked and felt like. I definitely had my favorite pieces, but those weren't until day two. As I wound down for the night, Brittany, the creative director, sent me some self-reflection exercises, more like journal prompts, to get me ready. To get me thinking of intentions, how I would carry myself if activated during our sessions, what I could anticipate showing up, such as stories or beliefs, and what physical responses I might expect if they did. This was a great exercise for my own personal awareness. Knowing before I walked in there what I could anticipate helped me to be prepared. I wrapped up for the night and although I was so tired, I was struggling to *turn off*. I knew this was just excitement, nerves... almost like the first day of school jitters. I remember starting my nightly prayer but before I was able to finish, I fell asleep.

How did the night fly by so fast? It feels like I just closed my eyes, I thought to myself as I woke naturally at 5:30 a.m. Then I suddenly realized, *Today is the day. Today is the day I take aligned action—that I move. My personal movement that is going to launch me into the next version of myself. Today I am granting myself permission to do me.* I got up and went full out. Water, shower, rechecking my luggage, ensuring I had all I needed for the day's production, and then contemplating breakfast. I heard Brittany's voice telling me I needed to make sure I ate breakfast because it was a packed day and I needed to be nourished. *I better go eat. Oh no, you don't, Candice. When you eat your belly bloats and puffs out; you don't want that look. Especially with the type of photoshoot you will be having today,* I told myself. I let that thought just sit there. I didn't judge it, just let it sit there. Then I walked myself through my fact-checker process.

- Candice: You know you need to eat to nourish yourself—*fact*. You know food restriction is an old habit you acted out to prove to yourself that your body, that you, weren't fat—*fact*.

I knew with both those facts that avoiding food was not of my highest good and would be reinforcing an old habit and pattern that did not serve me in this #meera. I needed to feel fueled, have energy, and continue to break patterning that was no longer serving me.

I headed down to the buffet and grabbed pineapples, strawberries, eggs, and two slices of turkey bacon. I filled up until I was satisfied then headed back to the room. As I was tuning my violin I got this instant thought, idea, message... *I need to journal.* An invitation to my inner child, giving her permission to come out. To play. To be bold. To be loud. To be all the things she was shamed for growing up. To join me in healing together. I got emotional writing to her. I saw her so clearly it was like she was sitting next to me on the bed, awaiting a hug. I thought to myself, *How frightened and alone she must have felt all these years. How protective she thought she was being for me over the years.*

It was time.

Shortly after, my makeup artist and hair stylist arrived. Bam, they went at it. They were such a spark of energy. Playfully loud, excited, gassing me up, and just sharing in my journey. They asked me questions about my book, which morphed into deeper story telling not only on my end but theirs. Not sure why I was so surprised to learn some of the similarities we all had as I know that when we meet people, it is never an accident. I felt so held and not an ounce of judgment as I shared my *why* of the book. I soaked in being on the receiving end... it felt so good to just *be*. These ladies were so talented. I felt the exact hype and confidence I needed going into this photoshoot.

I could feel excitement and anticipation building. I was feeling like I needed to take a shit but also knew it was just my nerves. The nervous shits—IBS in full swing. Sam, my publisher and storytelling director for this experience, picked me up at the hotel. We chit-chatted on the way, which felt nice, since my and Sam's relationship was typically shelved around my book process and things that surfaced in those in-between moments. I welcomed the casual and less-intense chat! We arrived, unloaded the car, and headed into the studio—and let's just say everything was divinely working out in my favor.

As the production team was getting all set up, I found myself walking around, taking in the room—where the door was, where my dresses would be hung, the activity of the photographer setting up, where the bathrooms were, and the directors finalizing ideas for flow. I kept finding myself in my head but then would quickly catch my thoughts, *Candice, breathe! Inhale ... hold... exhale ... hold. Connect, Candice—what messaging is your body sharing with you in this now moment?* After thirty minutes or so of setting up and deciding which part to capture first, it was time to get *buck-ass naked.* As I stood on the white cloth below me, naked, bare, fully vulnerable, and exposed in front of people I'd just met, Sam gently painted parts of me gold. Wrapped in a white sheet, keeping the moment and energy sacred, Sam guided me to the set, where the unraveling all began. The first thing rolling through my mind was my physical limitations as a result from my pelvic floor repair. Since that surgery my right hip socket has difficulty with certain ranges of motion. I was nervous how it would all look, the awkwardness of moving around. As I laid on the sheet being painted in gold, accenting my visible scars and stretch marks, I began to tell my story and the significance behind each. From four pregnancies (three to full term), a tubal ligation, two laparoscopies for my endometriosis, my pelvic organ prolapse, a partial hysterectomy, and a D&C from a miscarriage, I shared how each uniquely designed impression in my skin was actually a beautiful reflection of all my body had not only endured but carried me through.

As we shifted in positioning I could feel parts of my physical body shifting. My breast falling to the side, extra skin from my fifty-pound weight loss hanging at the abdomen, and my butt sticking to the sheet as I tried to reposition. I could feel myself tense up. *This must look awful from their view,* I told myself. *Candice, stop it. This is natural, it is beautiful. You get to decide beautiful, not society, not Keith, not your Dad, not any of your exes — YOU and only you. You just spoke in great detail about all your body has endured — you need to believe deep inside, every inch of you breeds beauty.* Deep inhale and exhale... *you are perfectly and wonderfully made,* I told myself over and over until the tension dissipated. Girls always know the good angles, the bad angles, and we all most definitely know our good side. And I must say it wasn't that I was concerned about what they thought of me and my body; I was concerned with how I looked. Again, my thoughts. My beliefs. Societal pressures have placed such unrealistic measures on individuals and how we are supposed to show up, look, and carry ourselves. The pressure is undeniably stressful. It feels like every week there is a new standard placed on us that feels so far out of reach... in fact, I have zero desire to reach for it. If that leaves me single forever because my appearance is too masculine looking and I am not firm and toned enough and wear wrinkles where I smile, well, looks like my #meera will be indefinite.

As we wrapped up for the day, I felt proud. I'd literally spent the majority of the shoot naked, scooting back and forth on the floor, side shots, top body shots; it was a proud moment and allowed me to see how much of myself I had healed. *NEVER* would I have even considered doing this even last year. When the vision came to me of doing it this way, I had to trust myself and go all in. I was scared up to the point it was time to remove my clothes. I got back to the hotel and was so exhausted. Mentally, emotionally, and physically drained. I wanted to go straight to bed but knew

I needed a bath, to journal on the day, and order room service… in that exact order. I plopped on the bed and just *was* for ten entire minutes. Realizing what I had accomplished, I allowed myself to sit in it, celebrating myself. I unpacked the luggage, washed all the makeup off my face, brushed my hair, took an extra long bath, ordered a cheeseburger, and prepped my clothes and luggage for day two. It felt so good to have all my boxes checked and to wind down for the night. Listening to Trevor Hall, eyes closed sitting on my bed, I grounded myself, feeling in full gratitude. *Candice, you did the effing thing. One of your biggest fears—being fully visible and seen—and you crushed it!* As I was enjoying the moment, my phone started pinging, pulling me out of the experience. I looked down on my phone to see Sam loading day one behind-the-scenes clips into our private team chat.

One by one the small clips loaded into the private group. One by one I viewed them to see exactly what Keith meant by, "It's not your face, it's your body." The stomach rolls while sitting, the thickness of my thighs, all of the parts I despised about me were the ones that stood out the most. As I sat there leaned up against the hotel headboard, tears fell. One by one they fell, streaming down my face. *Having the awareness of where my trigger point is will help me for tomorrow,* I thought. *It will also help me to gauge the work I am doing and still need to do. Candice, this is just data. You've got this. A work in progress, and one day at a time we move.* I was hoping I could partake in this experience and then walk out giving zero fucks, but the truth is, that's not realistic, and I do care. I care deeply. And it isn't others' views or opinions of my body. I mean, this team has hyped me up so much.

They have shared just how beautiful they see me from the inside out. *It's me.* It's me who has to get there. Don't you find it quite interesting how we latch onto the less-than-desirable things people share with us, but when they share something positive, there is disbelief and doubt?

Processing through journaling is a way I can speak to myself, data dump, and flow without judgment, meaning making, and criticizing myself. Those words have power. They allow me to see where I am and where I have the power to reframe, course correct, and build awareness of work that is still in progress. I felt it all. I allowed it all. I welcomed it all. Then what I did next is where I took my power back. I pulled up the video that was the most revealing and triggering and I forced myself to point out the things about it that made it beautiful. It wasn't easy, and it took a lot longer than I hope it will in the future. But the point is I allowed myself to see what others in the room saw that day. I allowed myself to see my body for all it has done for me. I quieted my husband's view of my physical body. I quieted my father's words of *fat fuck* and *beached whale.* I quieted my ex-boyfriend's voice calling me a "fat cunt bitch" while many months pregnant. I silenced them all. Instead I welcomed my voice. I invited in my voice. I allowed myself to say sorry. I laid in bed cradling and holding all parts of me, helping her to feel safe and loved.

I fell asleep cradling myself and before I knew it, it was 5:30 a.m. I woke feeling so refreshed, rested, and ready to see what day two was going to bring me. I immediately did my gratitudes and dropped into myself, feeling the warmth in my body as I acknowledged just how grateful I was for the women who had entered my life, supporting me through this, and the woman I was becoming. I started my day with water, showering, and doing my daily journaling practice. I was surprised by what I found myself writing: God, use me as your vessel. God, use me as the messenger. God, use me as the conduit of service to self. *Huh, that's weird,* I thought. I headed down to the lobby to meet the others. We loaded up and headed to the offsite destination for production day two.

Once we arrived we greeted each other with hugs. The scenery was so beautiful. I captured it on video but it surely didn't do it justice at all. Then moving around, I realized, of course, I needed to go to the bathroom. In good ole Candice fashion, I looked for a nice area where I could drop my pants and pee in nature. And, of course, Andee was also on the very same mission. I was like, THESE ARE MY PEOPLE. No second thoughts at all. I literally dropped down into a squat, leaning up against a rock as Sam shielded me with a sheet since I was more in the open than Andee. That's power. Not giving a shit. And also not giving a shit I pissed all over my leg and flip flops in the process. Water, anyone?

So, Reader, cancel the outside noise, their voice, your voice. Allow this chapter to serve as a permission slip. That if you, too, struggle with body image, don't allow it to drive you to deprive your physical body of what it needs to thrive—food, water, positive self-talk, all of which energetically supports your sacred vessel. We are all beautifully woven, unique in our own design. Your scars and stretch marks serve as impressions of your past. A remembering of your journey through life thus far. Flawlessness doesn't exist, anywhere. Know, Reader, that as I continue walking through my pain of becoming one with myself, that I witness you in your walk. If you have not been kind to your body. If you have talked down to it when all it has done is show up for you and held what you were not ready to face. Allow this chapter, my lived experience, to show you what is possible when you do *the work*.

PERMISSION GRANTED to face your fears and grow.

The Blooming Era

"When you step into your power, you begin to focus on what is over what was."

—Candice West

I am ready, I said to myself as the production crew and I walked to the destination, all of us carrying props, luggage, a violin, personal items, food, and snacks. We immediately looked at all the wardrobe outfits to see what was on the list first. These women didn't let me help much; they were emphasizing me not being the doer since that had been a theme in my life. It was all about me receiving, which I noticed felt good at times and uncomfortable during others. We found the perfect spot, the perfect tree. Settling in, I looked at all the beauty surrounding me. The animals, trees, wheatgrass, flowers, the gentle breeze hitting my face at the perfect time as I felt sweat bead up on my lip, the sun providing warmth, and the sky—it was absolutely breathtaking. The women in my company equally beautiful. I felt so much gratitude for these women. Seeing the energetic match between us felt so good. I know we call people into our lives who are on the same energetic level and frequency as us, or because they will serve as our teacher to help get us there. I felt honored to be with such amazing women.

"Alright, ladies," Sam said. "I thought we could sit here in a circle before we get started and share our intention for the day and if you feel called, something you want to share with Candice."

As she said that I noticed my stomach tighten up. *Oh, gosh, they are going to say things to me and about me,* I thought. This was one of the moments that didn't feel comfortable. I wasn't often given compliments or gassed up so I could feel the dis-ease in receiving whatever they were called to share. I could feel a softening as they shared around the circle. The words and the sentiments—well, I am leaving those to myself. The sacredness of the words and the deep emotion of heartfelt gratitude are for me. I sat in awe, wonder, and curiosity; it was like they were looking at and describing someone completely different.

We shifted our energy and after a twenty-minute embodiment practice, guided by Andee, we were dropped in and ready to get started. Out in the open, I stripped down and changed into my yellow dress. This was definitely a favorite of mine. I truly felt like a goddess earth angel in it. It was free flowing, vibrant; the color brought in the feelings and sensations of joy, the sleeves when my arms were fully extended looked like an angel. I just loved everything about it. Music blaring in the background, my hype team began instructing me to move... what a different energy than the day prior where it was a more embodied and sacred energy. Now, it was beautiful, but I was ready to move and bring out my inner child.

Speaking of inner child, this era of mine was not safe in any fashion. Not safe to be me, be seen, and so the white dress brought in the sacred energy of seeing myself for all I have been and am. After some fun flowy moves as the breeze hit my face, I laid down on my right side, cradling a mirror. I looked deeply at myself. *I see me, I see all of me. A softness, a femininity that is allowing itself to emerge. A femininity that has been hiding for many years and a welcoming and invitation that it is safe to show up and be seen.* Being so close to this mirror I could really see myself. The details and the curvature of my eyes, my nose, my lips, my chin. The small creases and wrinkles that meet my eyes and mouth as I smile. And then, as I stood boldly looking out into the meadow and mountains, I felt this sense of empowerment as if I had arrived.

The end was near! It was so hot, I was hungry, and we all still had so many ideas. What we did next would end my experience. It would be a wrap. Early on in the planning, I had shared with my team how I envisioned myself with roots in hand and dirt all over me. It was to symbolize my lived experiences through my various seasons. That we are always in a season of growth, evolution, and transformation. They brought my vision to life, and I could not have been happier with the outcome. And not the outcome as in photos, but the one inside. I was mentally, emotionally, and physically zapped. It was like everything had been excavated from within and fully exposed in my evolution, allowing me to keep what served and extract what didn't.

"And it's a wrap," Brittany shared as we took the final shots, hoping to have secured my book cover photo. These women were into this production like it was their own. I felt so held and supported, I had to keep myself from tearing up. I spent the remainder of the day processing and reflecting on the incredible day I'd had and how life-changing the experience was for me.

Getting back to my room, I immediately washed my face and hopped in the shower. I had dirt in every nook and cranny, and my hair was like a rat's nest from all the wind and dirt over the hours. It felt good to just stand there and take on the water and heat and just be. As I washed my body, I noticed where all the mud marks were. It was like a little impromptu ceremony. As I washed each mark of dirt, I imagined it as a remnant of energy, comments, and actions over time that I had tucked into my body. Stored emotions that had not yet been released, or maybe had been this week but still had some residue left behind. I thanked my body for showing up. For allowing myself to be vulnerable around strangers, now friends. For finally choosing me and seeing me for probably the first time ever. I spent the evening journaling, packing, and listening to music as I settled in for the evening. Alarm set, lights out—it's a wrap, Colorado.

I was up and at 'em at 3:15 a.m. for a 4:30 a.m. Uber. I showered, finished packing my toiletries, gulped a bottle of water down the hatch, put a journal page in my notes section, and I was out the door. With a much shorter ride to the airport, I found myself with my luggage checked and through security with a whole ninety minutes to spare. I stopped in a store to pick up a Celsius, water, pistachios, and trail mix for the day (I know—not quite fluffy eggs, bacon, and fresh fruit). From the store I found myself walking aimlessly around the airport. I noticed a bookstore so to kill some time I took a step in. I looked around at all the books on the shelves, the different classifications, even saw one for bestsellers. I thought to myself, *Oh, let me sit in the energy of what it would feel like to be a bestselling author. I'm gonna visualize my book, even though I have no clue what it looks like yet, on the shelf right here, right now.* I sat in the energy of what it could possibly feel like. My boys ask me all the time, "Mom, what if you got bestselling author?" And I always say to them, "That would be amazing. That means my story reached a lot of people. That means there's a lot of people who, if they choose themselves, can begin to heal. But even if it only reaches one person, I will have done my job."

As I moved about the airport, I suddenly heard it. *OMG, it's the song. Now? Of course,* I thought in sheer excitement. The Feather Theme from Forrest Gump. This song meant so much to me and my father. In high school my orchestra conductor had a cassette tape made of our spring concert; I still have it. My dad used to listen to that cassette all the time when he would drive downtown to Chicago for work. His favorite was the Feather Theme. This was the same song he walked me down the aisle to. I heard it so clearly. I kept walking, following the sound, hoping to get to a speaker where I could hear it louder and more clearly. But it seemed the more I walked the more the song faded; it eventually disappeared. The song was maybe halfway over and suddenly it was gone. I stood there so puzzled and confused. I felt sadness because I'd felt such a connection with my dad and I wasn't ready to let that go yet. Then, I noticed to the left of me the book store I had been in earlier. And then I felt in that instant, *Permission granted.* It was like he, my dad, was giving me permission from beyond that it was okay, I was okay, and he was proud of me. It was the closure I never got. It was like he knew I needed to write this book to heal me while also helping others. It was like he was granting me permission to tell the world my story regardless of who was going to approve. It was about me and my beliefs, my lived experiences, and how I was able to look at them as opportunities to move and take aligned action; to unravel, to evolve, to bloom.

I remember walking to the side of the airport and just bawling. I could feel him. And there was a message in his presence that I felt so deeply connected to. It's not about the outcome of the book; it's about the process, the unraveling, and this was just him granting me permission to let go. To stop punishing myself. As I caught my breath and wiped my tears, I made my way to my gate. As I stood there, I noticed four girls off to my right—volleyball players, actually. Their book bags with their team logo read, *Deeply Rooted*, another symbolic message for me as I closed out this sacred trip.

The return home was long. I was tired, my body was sore, and I was ready to sleep in my own bed. There was a torrential downpour and because of lightning it took us a while to deplane. Finally making it to baggage claim to retrieve all my luggage, my violin didn't arrive. It was missing. I started to feel myself panic, *This has been with me everywhere I have gone in my life since I was twelve years old*, I thought. Then a quick shift to just having a deep knowing that it would be okay, that it was here somewhere. I went to the baggage claim agent to figure out what was going on. After some research, it appeared my violin got misplaced due to the starting and stopping of the carousel from the lightning. They were able to locate my violin and retrieve it for me. When the airport employee handed me my violin I couldn't help but notice, and chuckle at, how it was covered in mud. *But how?* It was a true symbolic representation of the healing of my little girl within.

The following week, my somatic certification graduation and retreat led me into another deep expansion

I was not expecting. Releasing expectations welcomes the unknown. It welcomes the energy of desire, fun, and play. Detaching welcomes it all. I would be lying if I didn't mention I was a little nervous meeting these girls in person. They all had a long-term rapport with my mentor; I was the new girl. I knew what that felt like having moved around from school to school and duty station to duty station. It was always met with anxiety, fear of not being accepted, and self-judgment.

When I arrived I told myself in my rental car I was just going in as me. This me that has pulled off and broken all her masks she has worn throughout all the years. This me who is rooted in herself for the first time ever in her life. This me who is just going to bring along all parts of me: loud, obnoxious, opinionated, belching, farting, snorting, and a sensitive soul who just longs for connection and acceptance. I didn't know what to expect, but it was absolutely amazing. I detached from any expectations and met these beautiful women who all just welcomed me with a warm hug. And to be honest, this was the energy the entire weekend. No pedestals, no hierarchy, just love. No gossiping, no cattiness, no drama. It was powerful, and it really allowed me to plant the seed, *I am enough*, into my freshly excavated body.

I won't share all the details of the weekend as it is sacred but what I will share is the depth that Andee took me to, which welcomed me to close the loop of, *it's my fault*. You see, in this weekend's event we were also met with a full moon, which as Blair, a fellow sister and student, said highlighted the energies of the mother and father and ancestral beings and encouraged generational healing to occur. When she said that, I was like, *Ugh*, only because I knew it was the weekend of my father's four-year death-anniversary and I already had that on the forefront of my mind.

The following day, Friday, we all got to have an experience, as Andee titles it, *under the tree.* It is an extremely sacred experience and we are so very held and witnessed in whatever we are navigating. Well, wouldn't you know that after going no-contact with my mother in September the year prior, my mother left me a voicemail. *Seriously, Universe?* Of all the days, weekends, and even moments... she called just before we began our special sessions? *Could this be a coincidence?* I thought. I felt annoyed, to be honest. I was already navigating the heaviness of my dad's anniversary, and now my mom, after ten months of no-contact, called me. All I could think about was Blair's previous information regarding the full moon and how this was really happening... then Carl Jung's quote surfaced, *"What you resist persists."*

As I sat under the tree with my beautiful sisterhood sister, Tiffany, we began our special session together. I remember sharing how I had a tension headache and seeing my mom had called had made it worse. I was circulating thoughts that I was a bad daughter for going no-contact, should I give in, should I keep the boundary while I am still healing—all the questions flooded my internal cavity, leaving me overly annoyed because I wanted to be in the presence of these women, not thinking about my mother. Tiffany asked the most beautiful questions, witnessing me in my mess. Such a safe space and energy to be in. Continuing checking in and assessing my physical body and what it was speaking to me, I began noticing how I didn't want to do this wrong. I didn't want to repeat the pattern of my father. I felt such heaviness in my chest, quivering in my throat, and throbbing in my head.

As we wrapped up my session Tiffany had just a couple of questions. As we both looked over I could see the looks on the faces of everyone gathered. I responded to Tiffany's questions, saying I was annoyed with my mom, and that my uncertainty with how to proceed was rooted in what I was carrying about my father. Never getting closure with my dad and my mom as an addict, what if she were to overdose or pass on from natural causes before we could work through our issues? What if I didn't get closure with her as well? My mentor was able to show that deep down there was a loop that had not been closed between me and my father, so I was trying to avoid repeating it with my mom; that was the cause of my inner conflict.

In true Andee fashion, she offered me an invitation to dive deep into these feelings in an effort to close this loop that had been open for four years. Without disclosing all the details, she offered to witness me in "conversation" with my father.

"Is it okay if I just think it in my head?" I asked.

"Yes," she replied. "But what makes it feel safer for you to say it in your head versus out loud?"

"Because in my head it stays there," I said. Lightbulb moment... *stays there.* Yep—to torment myself. To punish myself. It was a seed planted by someone else's words that I allowed to take root and continuously watered over the last four years. I then realized I needed to speak these words out loud or I would continue to carry all this in my body. Sitting in the chair, trying to hold in the blubbering and bellows I wanted to release, I shared, *"I forgive you."* Crying in deep pain, I continued expressing. I let out a big bellow, one that felt like it had come from so far down in the pit of my soul that I just couldn't control it. The women all stood behind me, witnessing me. Gentle touches on my shoulders. Sniffling from them almost as though they felt my pain, and for some, maybe even resonated with it. Hearing Andee's soft voice reminding me I was safe and to connect with the sensations in my body… guiding me to fully be able to close this loop; these moments will be forever ingrained in my memory.

It was now time to face myself. To face my own truth. Looking at myself, I was to share words to this now moment version of me. All I could see was pain in the reflection. I am not even sure of the words I spewed, if any at all; I just know I bared it all on that deck, in front of women I'd just met, and on such a special day. I remember just feeling present—not numb or dissociated, but as quick as the emotions were heavy and present, they were gone. It was like the deep bellow was the root finally being excavated, finally leaving my body and giving me space to plant new seeds of purpose and possibility. New seeds that granted me permission to bloom into the healthiest version of me.

Again, people come into our lives for a reason, a season, or a lifetime. And in this season, I am truly grateful for all these women and the opportunities and perspectives they offered me over the weekend. They have all helped me weed my garden, and I am looking forward to what blooms in its place.

Full circle… I have come full circle. This chapter is one of blooming, realizing the negative beliefs planted and watered over time don't have to continue growing. But also a chapter of deep introspection. A discovery and connection of the body's way to hold space for you, to hold it all. When we allow ourselves to take an honest look into our thoughts, actions, and behaviors, some are so subtle and discreet you on your own might forever miss them. That simple, yet powerful question of Andee's led me to the realization of the internalized suffering and punishment I was perpetuating and would have continued otherwise. My body's way of communicating with me that something needed to leave, to exit so I could move into the wholeness and truth of who I am, was overlooked for years. Reader, it's time to get curious. What are you harboring that is ready to be excavated so you, too, can bloom into the most beautiful version of self?

PERMISSION GRANTED to recognize and celebrate your inner strengths.

The Self-Renaissance Era

"The most important relationship you can have is the one you have with yourself, the most important journey you can take is one of self-discovery."

—Aristotle

Delta Airlines, you nailed this saying: *paths taken create the stories we tell.*

So much of my childhood was a blur but over time, as I heal and shed layers of wounds and emotions, I discover new things to unpack, work through, and let go. I will say, the beauty is in *the knowing.* It offers me a sense of self-compassion and acceptance of self. It offers me the opportunity to connect with little Candice and show her safety and love. The ability to re-parent her and tell her with assertiveness and a full heart that nothing she blamed herself for was ever her fault. That she was always worthy, beautiful, smart, and never ever too much or not enough. Her needs were valid and real. The wholeness of who she was triggered those around her who had not yet had the courage to step forward and do *the work.* To seek self-discovery and move through the hardships, leaning on healthy anchors instead of behind painful words and actions.

It has been quite the healing journey and a slow unraveling. Through this process, I've discovered I've been a caregiver my entire life without anyone modeling what it looks like to care for myself. In fact, the caregiver in me was always celebrated by others, which reinforced that behavior. It was my goal to show others they were loved... and loved unconditionally, even if that meant sacrificing self in some way.

All my life I've felt undervalued, underappreciated, and definitely not accepted for who I am. I've felt invisible in a room full of people and misunderstood, and have questioned my purpose more than I care to admit. But how can I expect others to value, appreciate, and accept me when even my own thoughts, actions, and behaviors didn't show this? Service to self was obsolete. I watched my mom pour into men her whole life, never once putting herself first. It felt very much like she was searching for someone to fill her void. And here, all these years later, I have realized I have done the same. I have bounced from relationship to relationship, looking for a deep fairy-tale love but met with chaos, conflict, and self-sabotage. I seem to attract men who are also hurt and trying to find their way. Of course we would find each other, because we are reflections of one another's deepest wounds.

But, the key is first feeling fully worthy of yourself. Valuing and accepting yourself. It is then you can be in a place to call in the person created for all of you. I have learned this the long, hard, and painful way, my friends. My hope is that if you see yourself in this, even just a small story, that first you celebrate yourself for having that awareness. It's all a journey after that.

All this to say, it's time to tend to your garden, friends. The most important relationship that exists is the one with yourself. Everyone and everything else around you should just compliment you. Get to know your weeds and why they are there and keep spreading. Dig deep and excavate the roots that were planted and have been growing since the beginning of time. Nourish all of you with your fertilizer—*lived experiences*—using them as guideposts forward in curiosity and self-discovery.

I have spent what feels like my entire life seeking love and acceptance to feel worthy everywhere else but within. And it is within where, over these last several months, I have found peace. Where the chaos has quieted. Where I have really gotten to know myself and truly fallen in love with all parts of me, with her. The parts of me born on my given birthdate, and the parts of me birthed over time to keep me safe. I have found solace in knowing that while some of these parts no longer live actively in my mind driving my thoughts, actions, and behaviors, they are there lying dormant just in case I need them again.

But it is in the choosing. We have a choice to view our experiences from the lens of growth and perspective shifting, or maintain a victim-conscious mentality and remain stagnant. We all know what the soil looks and smells like when stagnation prevents the absorption of rainwater—the murky color, the odor permeating the surrounding area. Imagine what stagnation looks and feels like inside your internal cavity. It is in deciding to put your needs first. To no longer live in the mindset of service over self. And when we can pour into ourselves not only are we feeling fulfilled but we are modeling to our friends and family just how much we value self. That is the seed we want to plant, to take root, and water.

If you need a permission slip, someone to witness you in your mess, to help identify where you might be stagnant or where there is more room for excavation and expansion, I am here. I am here as a friend, peer, and someone who also knows what it is like to feel like they have made a mess out of their life. Allow me to witness you. Whatever roots are so deeply entangled under the soil, know it is not too late. I am proof! Know that there is nothing you have been through or done that cannot be unraveled. And also understand you cannot sit in the muck and expect flowers to bloom. Let's bring you back home to self. It is time to give yourself permission to tend to your garden.

"It's time to reverse ... to find my way back to the first seed planted. But first I must navigate my way through the intertwined roots that have been watered over many years. And when I get there, when I find it, I will honor it, thank it, and then excavate it.

Then…

I will plant my seed and become her. I will become a healthier, stronger, more empowered her. I will discover new things about her. I will discover new places to go and people to meet. I will discover her, outside of him, outside of them. And I will bloom again and again… as many times through as many seasons needed to become her. This becoming her feels heavy, hard, and impossible, but I crush impossible… I am proof impossible IS possible. Remember, seeds are planted everywhere ... it's the ones we choose to water that matter." —Candice West

PERMISSION GRANTED to live fully and authentically.

Your Little-Self Permission Slip

D ear Littlest _____,
I know you have been hiding out for so long. Waiting to be given permission that it is okay to laugh loudly, talk incessantly, belch disgustingly, dance freely. I know you have discounted your needs since you were a little child, likely because you were never really taught or shown how to have and express your needs, to have boundaries, or to nurture self. I know it hasn't felt safe your entire life. Judgment from those around you. Criticism from those who were supposed to accept you fully. Shamed because you were human and didn't know how to uncage yourself.

I want you to know, littlest _____, today is the day. Today you are coming out fully. To be seen, to be witnessed, to be loved fully for who you are and all the parts that have been birthed over the years to provide you safety and protection. We are going to thank them all. One by one. Then we are going to let them go elsewhere. Let them know that the driver's seat is now occupied by me, the older version of you. That today, we are going to merge and blend. We are going to unify into one.

I have you. We can hold space for one another. It is a mighty, beautiful thing. Together we are going to heal part of you, littlest _____. We are going to heal and cross many timelines and beyond as we join forces. Know I have you. There will be times I tap into you as well for the play, fun, creative flow you offer me. We will lean on one another in these new now moments creating something magical.

Just know, if you feel scared, timid, fearful, or anything that is not woven in peace and love, that it is normal and we will work through it together. You might find yourself retreating; this is also normal. You have been forced through many entities in life to hide for safety. To show up wearing masks to feel safe. Know that I will be your permission slip to still come out of hiding. To still show up boldly.

I have you. We have each other.

I can't wait to journey and heal together,

Love always, Older _____

Your Present-Day Permission Slip

D ear Present Day Self _____,
This is your permission slip to come as you are, welcoming all versions and parts of self, past and present. This journey called life doesn't always offer us the safety to be wholly and unapologetically ourselves.

Self-abandonment is a silent thief. It creeps in when we dismiss our feelings, silence our inner voice, or hide parts of ourselves out of fear, shame, judgment, or embarrassment. This act of turning away from our true selves creates a gap—a void that leaves us feeling disconnected and unfulfilled.

But here's the truth: we have the power to close that gap. We have the power to reclaim every fragment of our being, to stand tall in our vulnerabilities, and to embrace our entire essence.

And it all starts with permission. So, here is your permission slip. A sacred commitment to self.

This permission slip is a powerful document, a tangible reminder that you have the right to be exactly who you are. You have the right to:

1. *Acknowledge Your Feelings*: Feelings are not weaknesses; they are signals from your soul. Allow

yourself to feel joy, sadness, anger, and fear. Each emotion is valid and part of your human experience.

2. *Embrace Your Past:* Your past, with all its trials and triumphs, has shaped you into who you are today. Embrace your journey, including the moments of shame and embarrassment, as they hold the lessons that guide your evolution.

3. *Honor Your Needs:* Your needs are important. You deserve to have them met. Whether it's rest, connection, or solitude, give yourself permission to prioritize your well-being.

4. *Speak Your Truth:* Your voice matters. Speak your truth, even if it trembles. Your authenticity has the power to inspire and liberate others.

5. *Celebrate Your Uniqueness:* There is no one else like you. Celebrate your quirks, talents, and dreams. Your uniqueness is your greatest gift to the world.

By signing this permission slip, you are making a profound commitment to yourself. You are declaring that you are worthy of love, respect, and acceptance —just as you are. You are stepping into your power, not despite your imperfections, but because of them.

As you sign and date this permission slip, let it serve as a constant reminder that you are enough.

_____   _____

Date   **Name**

Acknowledgments

To my parents for doing the best they could with what they knew at the time. Though I share my stories, it does not take away from the deep love and gratitude I have for you. It all had to happen in this way. Thank you for signing up in this lifetime to offer me the lessons I needed to heal this time around.

To the many mentors over the years giving me a safe space to share, a permission slip to cry, scream, even be in denial, and the unconditional love of me as a person, I could not be where I am without you all.

If you're interested in learning more about Candice's courses and coaching, supportive tools, and free resources, or if you're looking for a keynote speaker for your next event, please visit:

www.candicewest.com

You can also email candice@candicewest.com.

Be sure to follow @candice_west on Instagram.

About the Author

Candice West, the creator of Just PIVOT, Rooted In Fear, and the BLOOM Methodology, is a multi-modality somatic embodiment coach and retired Navy nurse with twenty-two years of service. Since overcoming her own struggles with self-sabotage and self-abandonment, she is now on a mission to support women to reclaim their wholeness of SELF. She emphasizes the importance of proactive change coupled with self-love, self-care, self-compassion, and self-connection to shift from a place of service of others to service to self.